Contents

Contents

Grammar Rules!

High-Interest Activities for Practice and Mastery of Basic Grammar Skills

Grades 1-2

by Jillayne Prince Wallaker

Dedication

With lots of love to Maegen, Madalen, Ian, and always to Willie.

Credits

Editors:
Tracy Soles, Donna Walkush

Layout Design:
Victory Productions, Inc.

Illustrations:
Janet Armbrust

Cover Design:
Peggy Jackson

This book has been correlated to state, national, and Canadian provincial standards. Visit *www.carsondellosa.com* to search for and view its correlations to your standards.

ISBN 0-88724-975-2

▶ Introduction

Some teachers, parents, and students might be surprised by the title *Grammar Rules!* However, this grammar book was developed so that writing teachers can show students that grammar can be understood (and sometimes even fun) when presented in a clear, reasonable way. *Grammar Rules!* builds on each topic in a logical progression so that students learn the facts behind the skill, practice the skill, then are able to put their new grammar knowledge into action.

After each grammar skill is introduced, plenty of practice is provided, along with a Review Work and a Draft Book exercise for students to transfer their new skill. Review Work assignments focus on previously covered skills or provide additional practice with a skill on the given page. The Draft Book assignments encourage students to apply the grammar skills beyond the reproducible pages and incorporate them into their own writing. For the Draft Book activities, students can complete assignments on loose-leaf paper in a folder or in a spiral or composition notebook.

Each grammar skill presented in the Review Work and Draft Book exercises has a locator code, such as underlining nouns with yellow. This code is consistent throughout the book. This provides a student with a patterned tool for self-monitoring as well as self-editing.

This book also contains a comprehensive review on pages 114–115. These pages are perfect for a pre-lesson and post-lesson assessment or an end-of-year test.

A Student Editing Checklist is included on page 116. This page is designed to be used as a self-editing tool. By assigning two or three items to check at a time, students are not overwhelmed with "getting everything right," but instead can focus on very specific skills until they understand them completely. Once mastery of the selected editing skills is evident, an additional set of items can be assigned. The same piece of student writing can be used for several editing assignments or students can use different writing samples. This convenient checklist can be kept with each student Draft Book as a reminder of grammatical variations that can be included in their writing. It can also be used to monitor student progress by dating each skill when it is demonstrated consistently.

Grammar Rules! will quickly become a resource that writing teachers return to for strong grammar activities to show their students that grammar really does rule!

Name _____

▶ People

Nouns are words that name people.
    examples: brother, teacher
    examples: Corey, Dana

Write the names of six people in your class. Each of these names is a noun.

_____   _____

_____   _____

_____   _____

Use some of the nouns you listed to finish the sentences.

_____ is a girl.

_____ is a boy.

_____ has red hair.

_____ likes to read.

_____ is my friend.

 Review Work

Write the names of two people in your family. These are nouns, too!

_____   _____

✏️ **Draft Book**

Write three sentences using nouns that name people. Underline these nouns with yellow.

Name _____

Places

Nouns are words that name people. Nouns also name places.
examples: garage, jungle
examples: Grand Canyon, Australia

Circle the nouns that name places.

Jan	bear	cat	Hawaii
scissors	dime	school	truck
France	plate	store	United States
home	classroom	music	bird

Write the nouns that name places.

The pool is in the backyard. _____

The cat ran to the barn. _____

George drove to Toronto. _____

Stevie's class went to the zoo. _____

Max lives on Pine Street. _____

 Review Work

Find the nouns in the sentences that name people. Underline them with yellow.

Draft Book

Write three sentences using nouns that name places. Underline these nouns with yellow. Draw a triangle above each of these nouns.

© Carson-Dellosa

▶ Things

Nouns are words that name people and places. Nouns also name things.
   examples: bird, buttons
   examples: Yankee Stadium, Statue of Liberty

The nouns below name things. Draw a picture of each one.

	book	pencil	
	dog	shoe	

Use the nouns to finish the sentences.

Meg can write with a _____ .

Ian likes to read his _____ .

Caleb's _____ barked at the man.

Natalia put the _____ on her foot.

🔎 Review Work

Find the nouns in the sentences that name people. Underline them with yellow.

✏️ Draft Book

Write three sentences using nouns that name people, places, or things. Underline these nouns with yellow.

Name _____

▶ ABC Order

nouns

Nouns are words that name people, places, or things.

Look at the word pairs. Circle the noun in each pair.

home / hurry	boy / begin	do / door
library / lay	egg / eat	in / ice
Grandma / great	ant / and	for / farm
keep / king	could / cave	join / Jack

Write one of the first 12 letters of the alphabet in order in each box. Write each noun from the word pairs next to the letter it starts with. Now, the nouns are in ABC order.

☐ _____   ☐ _____

☐ _____   ☐ _____

☐ _____   ☐ _____

☐ _____   ☐ _____

☐ _____   ☐ _____

☐ _____   ☐ _____

 Review Work

Find the circled nouns that name things
in the word pairs. Underline them with yellow.

✎ Draft Book

Write six nouns. Your nouns should name people, places, and
things. Rewrite the nouns in ABC order.

▶ Finish the Alphabet ▶ nouns

Nouns are words that name people, places, or things.
Look at the words. Circle each noun.

old	are	quilt	running	say	singer	put	Wisconsin
the	zoo	X ray	teacher	hot	upstairs	rice	neighbor
yak	ask	mother	Patricia	tell	outside	born	Vermont

Start with M and write the last 14 letters of the alphabet. Write one letter in each box. Write each noun from above next to the letter it starts with. Now, the nouns are in ABC order.

🔍 **Review Work**

Find the circled nouns that name places.
Draw a triangle above each of these nouns.

✏️ **Draft Book**

Find a page of your writing.
Underline the nouns in yellow. Write the nouns in ABC order.

▶ Categories

Nouns are words that name people, places, or things.

Write each noun in the correct category.

ear	sister	gum
doll	baby	car
Dad	store	playground
Earth	foot	child
doctor	forest	classroom

People	**Places**	**Things**
_____	_____	_____
_____	_____	_____
_____	_____	_____
_____	_____	_____
_____	_____	_____

🔍 **Review Work**

Choose one list from above. Write the nouns in ABC order.

1._____   2._____   3._____

4._____   5._____

 Draft Book

Write three sentences using one noun from each category. Underline the nouns with yellow.

Name _____

▶ Find the Nouns

Nouns are words that name people, places, or things.

Underline the nouns.

Kira has a yellow sun on her shirt.

Chase went to the store to buy apples.

Her brother watered the plants on the deck.

Sabena placed the cupcakes on the counter.

The bike on the sidewalk belongs to my friend.

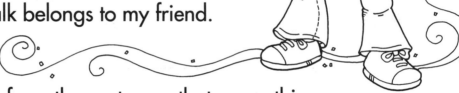

🔍 **Review Work**

Choose two nouns from the sentences that name things.
Draw a picture of each one. Write their names.

_____   _____

✏️ **Draft Book**

Make a list of the places you go during the week. Start with your home. These words are all nouns!

▶ Who Did That?

nouns

Nouns are words that name people, places, or things.

Draw an X on each word that is not a noun.

student   dripping   carpenter   doctor   more   over   librarian

walked   firefighter   teacher   write   clerk   chef   or

Use some of the nouns to finish the sentences.

The _____ gave Tonya a checkup.

The _____ built a new house for Audrey.

The _____ helps Ross measure with a ruler.

The _____ cooked the food in the restaurant.

The _____ helps Rita check out books.

The _____ put out the fire in the building.

🔍 **Review Work**

Find the other nouns in the sentences. Underline them with yellow.

✏️ **Draft Book**

Two of the nouns were not used
in the sentences. Write a sentence
with each one.

Name _____

Nouns are words that name people, places, or things.

Which nouns could you find in your desk at school? Draw a line from these nouns to the desk.

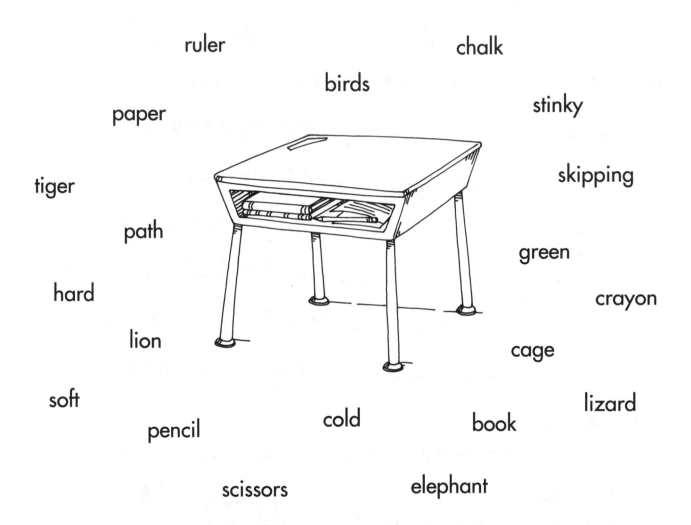

ruler   chalk

birds

paper   stinky

tiger   skipping

path   green

hard   crayon

lion   cage

soft   lizard

pencil   cold   book

scissors   elephant

🔍 **Review Work**

Underline the nouns that you could find at a zoo.

✏️ **Draft Book**

Write four sentences about your favorite part of the school day. Underline all of the nouns with yellow.

Name _____

▶ Names

A person's first and last names are proper nouns. Proper nouns name specific people, places, and things. A proper noun always starts with an uppercase letter.

Underline the proper nouns.

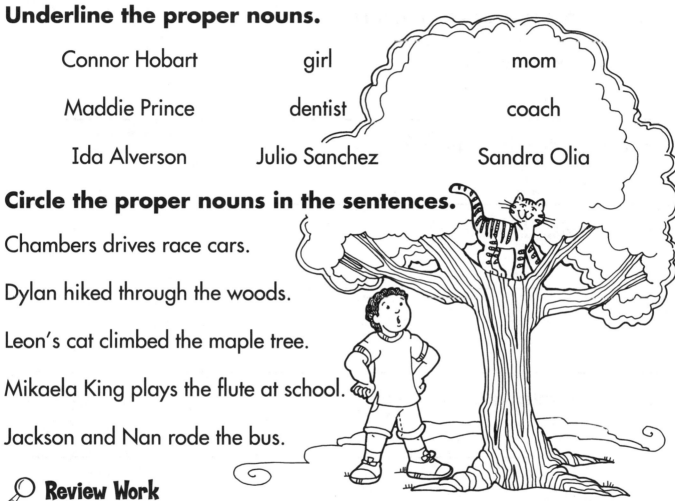

Connor Hobart	girl	mom
Maddie Prince	dentist	coach
Ida Alverson	Julio Sanchez	Sandra Olia

Circle the proper nouns in the sentences.

Chambers drives race cars.

Dylan hiked through the woods.

Leon's cat climbed the maple tree.

Mikaela King plays the flute at school.

Jackson and Nan rode the bus.

🔍 **Review Work**

Find the other nouns in the sentences. Underline them with yellow. Draw a triangle above each noun that names a place.

✏️ **Draft Book**

Write three sentences with a proper noun in each one.

Name _____

▶ Put Those Titles On ▶ proper nouns

A person's first and last names are proper nouns. Proper nouns also include titles, like Mr., Mrs., Miss, Ms., and Dr. A proper noun always starts with an uppercase letter.

Rewrite the sentences correctly.

Is ms. smith your teacher?

_____

cameron kendell, sr. is my father.

_____

Did deidre visit dr. molnar?

_____

leo marion, jr. is leo's full name.

_____

mr. and mrs. otten are her parents.

_____

 Review Work
   Underline all of the nouns in the sentences with yellow.

 Draft Book
   Write four sentences. Include a proper noun and a title in each one.

Name _____

▶ Pick and Fix

A person's first and last names and titles are proper nouns. The specific names of people, places, and things are all proper nouns. A proper noun always starts with an uppercase letter.

Circle the proper noun in each set of words. Rewrite the proper nouns correctly.

the park / mullen park   _____

lake huron / a lake   _____

my state / north carolina   _____

new york / her city   _____

the doctor / dr. beth calhoun   _____

mrs. oltoff / his mother   _____

meg michaels / my friend   _____

my street / transil street   _____

 Review Work

Draw an X next to each proper noun that names a person. Draw a triangle above each proper noun that names a place.

Draft Book

Write five sentences using proper nouns. Underline these nouns with yellow.

Name _____

# ▶ Addresses

Proper nouns name specific people, places, and things. A proper noun always starts with an uppercase letter. When proper nouns name a city and state, a comma goes between them.
  example: Orlando, Florida

Write the names and addresses correctly. Capitalize the proper nouns. Put a comma between each city name and state name.

mr. cody stoneson
461 oak avenue
littletown ohio 12345

_____

_____

_____

dr. coral sargasso
876 waterway boulevard
kelp maine 13579

_____

_____

_____

🔍 **Review Work**

Draw an X next to each proper noun that names a person.

✏️ **Draft Book**

Write your name and address. Capitalize all of the proper nouns. Put a comma between the names of your city and state.

▶ Special Times

proper nouns

Days, months, and holidays are proper nouns. A proper noun always starts with an uppercase letter.

Look at the words. Cross out the first letter of each proper noun and write an uppercase letter above it.

st. patrick's day	monday	thanksgiving
presents	sunday	july
new year's day	august	hearts
hanukkah	turkey	january
saturday	february	christmas
october	calendar	november
tuesday	leprechaun	december
wednesday	valentine's day	thursday

🔍 Review Work

Write a sentence about your favorite month or holiday.

_____

_____

✏️ Draft Book

Write two sentences using nouns that name days, months, and holidays. Underline these nouns with yellow.

Name _____

▶ Shortened Words proper nouns

Days and months are proper nouns. Some of these nouns can be abbreviated, or shortened. The complete words and their abbreviations always start with uppercase letters.

Draw lines to match the nouns that name days and months to their abbreviations. (Some months do not have abbreviations.)

Tuesday	Thurs.	January	Sept.
Friday	Sat.	February	Apr.
Sunday	Tues.	March	Oct.
Thursday	Fri.	April	Dec.
Wednesday	Sun.	August	Jan.
Monday	Wed.	September	Aug.
Saturday	Mon.	October	Mar.
		November	Feb.
		December	Nov.

🔍 Review Work

Starting with Sunday, write the days of the week in order. Start each word with an uppercase letter.

1._____ 2._____ 3._____

4._____ 5._____ 6._____

7._____

✏️ Draft Book

Write four sentences using nouns that name days and months. Use some abbreviations. Underline these nouns and their abbreviations with yellow.

20 CD-4337 Grammar Rules! Grades 1–2

Name _____

Make It Singular

A noun can be singular (one person, place, or thing) or plural (more than one). Usually, a noun becomes plural by adding an *s* to the end. Sometimes, a noun becomes singular by removing the *s* at the end.

Make the plural nouns singular. Use the nouns to finish the sentences. Decide if the plural or singular noun works best in each sentence.

balloons _____

    Kay has one blue _____ .

    Val has two red _____ .

shirts _____

    Pete has three striped _____ .

    Reba has one dotted _____ .

spots _____

    Gina's dog has a brown _____ .

    Dan's dog has four black _____ .

 **Review Work**

Find the other nouns in the sentences. Underline them with yellow.

Draft Book

Write a story about balloons or dogs. Underline the nouns with yellow. Circle the plural nouns.

Name _____

 # Lots of Shapes > **plural nouns**

A noun can be singular (one person, place, or thing) or plural (more than one). Usually, a noun becomes plural by adding an *s* to the end.

Make the nouns plural. Add to each picture to show more than one shape.

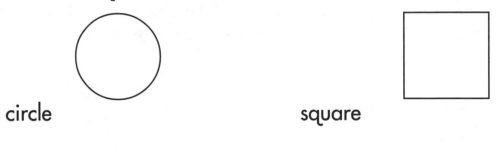

circle

_____

square

_____

triangle

_____

oval

_____

 Review Work

Write the plural nouns in ABC order.

1. _____   2. _____

3. _____   4. _____

 Draft Book

Make these nouns plural: rectangle, star, diamond, octagon.

Name _____

▶ Critters

A noun can be singular (one person, place, or thing) or plural (more than one). Usually, a noun becomes plural by adding an *s* to the end.

Make the nouns plural.

bee _____

frog _____

turtle _____

dog _____

snail _____

Use the plural nouns to finish the sentences.

Two _____ were sitting on a log.

Three _____ visited the flower.

Four _____ were on lily pads.

Five _____ were on the ground.

Six _____ were barking at cats.

🔍 **Review Work**

Find the other nouns in the sentences. Underline them with yellow.

✏️ **Draft Book**

Write a story about frogs jumping over a log. Underline the nouns with yellow.

▶ Party Time ▶ plural nouns

A noun can be singular (one person, place, or thing) or plural (more than one). Sometimes, a noun becomes plural by adding *es* to the end.

example: beach → bea**ches**   **example:** brush → bru**shes**

example: dress → dres**ses**   **example:** ax → ax**es**

Make the nouns plural by adding *es* to the end.

box _____   wish _____

dish _____   glass _____

Use the plural nouns to finish the sentences.

A magic frog gave Dante three _____ .

Dante wished for ten _____ of ice cream.

He also wished for ten _____ of milk.

His last wish was for ten _____ of cookies.

Now, Dante will have a party!

🔍 **Review Work**

Find the other nouns in the sentences. Underline them with yellow.

✏️ **Draft Book**

Write a story about a party you have been to. Underline the nouns with yellow. Circle the plural nouns.

Name _____

► Nature Walk

A noun can be singular (one person, place, or thing) or plural (more than one). Sometimes, a noun becomes plural by adding *es* to the end.

example: beach → beaches   **example:** brush → brushes

example: dress → dresses   **example:** ax → axes

Make the nouns plural by adding *s* or *es* to the end.

bird _____

fox _____

horse _____

flower _____

bush _____

bug _____

peach _____

tree _____

branch _____

plant _____

Review Work

Choose a noun from the list. Write the singular form on the first line and the plural form on the second line. Draw a picture to show each word.

_____   _____

Draft Book

Write a story about a time you went on a walk outside. Underline the nouns with yellow. Circle the plural nouns.

▶ Change the Ys

plural nouns

A noun can be singular (one person, place, or thing) or plural (more than one). Sometimes, a noun that ends in *y* becomes plural by changing the *y* to an *i* and adding *es* to the end.

example: party → part**ies**   **example:** city → cit**ies**

Make the nouns plural by changing the *y* to an *i* and adding *es* to the end.

baby _____   fly _____

penny _____   berry_____

story_____

Use the plural nouns to finish the sentences.

Jordan waved the _____ away .

Mitchell traded five _____ for a nickel.

Sasha ate three red _____ .

The boys read many _____ .

Lindley saw the _____ in the nursery.

🔍 Review Work

Find the other nouns in the sentences. Underline them with yellow.

✏️ Draft Book

Make these nouns plural: pony, buddy, cherry, and bunny. Use the nouns to write four sentences. Circle the plural nouns. Draw a star next to each singular noun.

Name _____

▶ Tricky Nouns

A noun can be singular (one person, place, or thing) or plural (more than one). Some nouns become plural by making changes in the middles or at the ends.

Draw lines to match the singular and plural nouns.

goose	children
mouse	people
tooth	feet
child	leaves
foot	women
person	mice
man	geese
woman	halves
leaf	men
half	teeth

Circle the tricky nouns in the sentences.

We cut the candy bars into halves.

Men, women, and children are all people.

A goose has two feet. Four geese have eight feet.

Mice have sharp teeth.

Many leaves are on that tree.

 Review Work
Find the other nouns in the sentences. Underline them with yellow.

✏ **Draft Book**
Write a story using some of the nouns above. Circle the plural nouns. Draw a star next to each singular noun.

Name _____

Use the plural form of the nouns to fill in the sentences.

example: penny   cup

There are six <u>pennies</u> in the two <u>cups</u>.

mouse   room

There are two_____ in the three _____.

child   bench

There are four _____ on the two _____.

blueberry   dish

There are five _____ in the two _____.

nut   box

There are six _____ in the four_____.

🔍 **Review Work**
Make these nouns plural: church, brush, fairy.

_____

✏️ **Draft Book**
Write a story using some of the nouns above. Circle the plural nouns. Draw a star next to each singular noun.

Name _____

▶ Choose a Noun

A noun can be singular (one person, place, or thing) or plural (more than one).

Circle the correct noun in each sentence.

The three (school, schools) are on the same street.

Two (cat, cats) climbed up the tree.

The (crab, crabs) has sharp claws.

Many (bush, bushes) have berries on them.

There are two (Julio, Julios) in my class.

That (boy, boys) waved at you.

One (doctor, doctors) left for the day.

A (tree, trees) can have many leaves on it.

🔍 **Review Work**

Find the other nouns in the sentences.
Underline them with yellow. Draw an X next to each proper noun.

✏️ **Draft Book**

Write a story using singular and plural nouns. Underline the nouns with yellow.

Name _____

▶ Mine, All Mine   possessive nouns

A possessive noun shows that something belongs to someone. Usually, a noun becomes possessive by adding 's to the end.

Finish each sentence with a possessive noun. The first one has been done for you.

The game belongs to my brother. It is my <u>brother's</u> game.

The pencils belong to Li. Those are _____ pencils.

That necklace belongs to Mom. It is _____ necklace.

The pennies belong to Juan. Those are _____ pennies.

That horse belongs to Rosa. It is _____ horse.

The hamster belongs to Tito. It is _____ hamster.

 Review Work

Write two singular and two plural nouns from the sentences above.

singular nouns   plural nouns

_____   _____

_____   _____

 **Draft Book**

Choose three friends. Use possessive nouns to write sentences about things that belong to them. Write one sentence about each friend.

Name _____

▶ Family Fun

A verb tells what someone or something is doing.
  example: The boy **swings** the golf club.
  example: The car **races** around the racetrack.

Underline the verbs in blue.

My sister Emily slides down the slide.

My dad pushes Paige on the merry-go-round.

My brother Hal climbs the big tree.

My grandmother sits on the bench.

My grandfather hits the ball with a racket.

My mom catches Emily at the bottom.

I swing across the monkey bars.

🔍 **Review Work**

  Underline the nouns in the sentences with yellow.

✏️ **Draft Book**

  Find a page in your Draft Book with the nouns underlined
  with yellow. Underline the verbs with blue.

Name _____

From the Sky

A verb tells what someone or something is doing.

Use the verbs to finish the sentences.

blew	boomed	burns	drifted
fall	flashed	shine	soaked

The sun _____ my nose.

The thunder _____ .

Rain _____ the sidewalk.

Lightning _____ across the sky.

The wind _____ our kites.

The clouds _____ across the sky.

Snowflakes _____ from the clouds.

Many stars _____ in the night sky.

 Review Work

Underline the nouns in the sentences with yellow.
Circle the plural nouns.

 Draft Book

Find a page in your Draft Book with the nouns underlined
with yellow. Underline the verbs with blue.

At the Circus

A verb tells what someone or something is doing.

Underline the verbs in the sentences. Draw a line from each sentence to the picture it matches.

The clown gives balloons to the children.

The seals balance balls on their noses.

The man sells treats like cotton candy.

Review Work

Underline the nouns in the sentences with yellow. Draw a star above each singular noun.

Draft Book

Find a page in your Draft Book with the nouns underlined with yellow. Underline the verbs with blue.

Name _____

► More "Doing" Words

A verb is a word that tells what someone or something is doing.

Underline each verb.

My teeth crunch the carrots.

The ice melts in the sun.

The sprinklers spray water on the lawn.

The kite soars above the clouds.

Virginia cuts with scissors.

The canoes float in the water.

Choose two sentences. Draw a picture to show each one.

 **Review Work**

Underline the nouns in the sentences with yellow. Circle the plural nouns.

✏ **Draft Book**

Use one of the sentences to write a story. Underline the verbs with blue.

Name _____

► Moving Animals   verbs

A verb is a word that tells what someone or something is doing.

Draw a box around each verb in the sentences. Underline the noun right before each verb.

A kangaroo hops.   The frogs jump.

A snake slithers.   The dog barks.

The kittens scratch.   The horses gallop.

The monkey swings.   The crabs pinch.

Write two plural nouns and their verbs from the sentences.

_____   _____

Write two singular nouns and their verbs from the sentences.

_____   _____

Which verbs have an *s* at the end? Circle the answer.

verbs with singular nouns   verbs with plural nouns

Review Work

Draw a star above each singular noun in the sentences. Circle the plural nouns.

Draft Book

Rewrite the sentences with plural nouns. What do you notice about the verbs in these sentences? Write a sentence to explain your answer.

Name _____

Sweet Stuff — noun and verb agreement

A singular noun uses a verb that has an *s* at the end. A plural noun uses a verb that does not have an *s* at the end.

    example: The **firefighter climbs** the ladder. (singular noun and verb)
    example: The **firefighters climb** the ladder. (plural noun and verb)

Circle the correct verb in each sentence.

Serena (plant, plants) the seeds.

The seeds (grow, grows) into flowers.

The bees (visit, visits) the flowers.

The bees (fly, flies) back to the hive.

The bees (make, makes) honey.

The beekeeper (collect, collects) the honey.

The grocery store (sell, sells) the honey.

Serena's father (buy, buys) honey.

The children (eat, eats) the honey on bread.

Review Work
Underline the nouns in the sentences with yellow.

Draft Book
Use one of the sentences to write a story. Underline the verbs with blue. Underline the nouns with yellow.

Name _____

 **Sea Life** — **noun and verb agreement**

A singular noun uses a verb that has an *s* at the end. A plural noun uses a verb that does not have an *s* at the end.

example: The girl **runs** in the race. (singular noun and verb)

example: The girls **run** in the race. (plural noun and verb)

Use the verbs to finish the sentences. Add an *s* to the ends of the words if needed.

crawl   hide   jump   snap   swim

The three dolphins _____ out of the water.

The eel _____ behind the rocks.

A fish _____ through the water.

The clams _____ their shells shut.

The crab_____ across the ocean floor.

🔍 **Review Work**

Underline the nouns in the sentences with yellow. Draw a star above each singular noun.

✏️ **Draft Book**

Write a story about a sea creature. Underline the verbs with blue. Underline the nouns with yellow.

Name _____

A singular noun uses a verb that has an *s* at the end. A plural noun uses a verb that does not have an *s* at the end.

example: The cat **meows** at my brother. (singular noun and verb)

example: The cats **meow** at my brother. (plural noun and verb)

Choose the correct noun and verb to finish each sentence. Write the words on the lines.

That _____ _____ loudly.

girl / girls   yell / yells

The three _____ _____ a pretty song.

bird / birds   sings / sing

Those _____ _____ at the children.

dog / dogs   barks / bark

A _____ _____ when it falls.

glass / glasses   crash / crashes

That _____ _____ well.

boy / boys   whistle / whistles

🔍 **Review Work**

Underline the nouns in the sentences with yellow. Circle the plural nouns.

✏️ **Draft Book**

Write a story about noises. Underline the verbs with blue. Underline the nouns with yellow. Make sure your nouns and verbs agree.

▶ Let's Exercise past and present tense

Verbs use tenses to tell when something is happening. When the action happens now, it is present tense. When the action happened before, it is past tense. One way to make a verb past tense is to add *ed* to the end.

Underline the present tense verb in the first sentence. Add *ed* to make the verb past tense in the second sentence.

The boys play baseball.

Last week, the boys _____ baseball.

The girls walk to the park.

Yesterday, the girls _____ to the park.

The players kick the soccer ball.

In the last game, the players _____ the soccer ball.

The runners race to the finish line.

An hour ago, the runners _____ to the finish line.

🔍 **Review Work**
Circle the plural nouns in the sentences.

✏️ **Draft Book**
Find a story you wrote. Draw a box around each verb with an *ed* ending.

▶ Cooking
past and present tense

Verbs use tenses to tell when something is happening. When the action happens now, it is present tense. When the action happened before, it is past tense. One way to make a verb past tense is to add *ed* to the end. If the noun is singular, take off the *s* or *es* at the end of the verb before adding *ed*.

Underline the present tense verb in the first sentence. Add *ed* to make the verb past tense in the second sentence.

Grandma bakes great cookies.

Last week, Grandma _____ brownies.

Grandpa grills hamburgers.

Yesterday, Grandpa _____ hot dogs.

Dad rolls the dough for cinnamon rolls.

Last night, Dad _____ the dough for cookies.

Mom mixes the batter for pancakes.

Last Tuesday, Mom _____ the fruit salad.

🔍 **Review Work**

Draw a star above each singular noun in the sentences.

✏️ **Draft Book**

Find a story you wrote. Draw a box around each verb with an *ed* ending.

▶ Verb Tenses   past and present tense

Verbs use tenses to tell when something is happening. When the action happens now, it is present tense. When the action happened before, it is past tense.

Circle the correct verb in each sentence.

Orlando (brushes, brush, brushed) his dog yesterday.

In the past, the glue (dried, dries, dry) quickly.

Mia (save, saved, saves) pennies for almost a year.

Last week, we (pick, picks, picked) blueberries.

He (flattens, flattened, flatten) the clay to make the project.

Trey (collected, collects, collect) 100 toy cars last year.

Anna and Courtney (tie, ties, tied) their shoes before they played.

Last summer, the sprinklers (waters, watered, water) the grass.

🔍 Review Work

Underline the nouns in the sentences with yellow.

✏️ Draft Book

Choose one of the sentences and write a story. Use some verbs with *ed* endings. Draw a box around each verb with an *ed* ending. Underline any other verbs with blue.

▶ Tricky Verbs ▷ other past tense verbs

Verbs use tenses to tell when something is happening. One way to make a verb past tense is to add *ed* to the end. Some verbs become past tense by making other changes.

example: The kitten **drinks** the milk. (present)
example: The kitten **drank** the milk. (past)

Read each sentence and write the correct past tense verb on the line.

Freda _____ to the mailbox.
runned, ran

Sydney _____ the flowerpot.
broke, breaked

Jada _____ in the pool.
swimmed, swam

Ricco _____ down the slide.
slid, slided

Will _____ his lunch box at school.
leaved, left

Ernest _____ a letter.
wrote, writed

🔍 **Review Work**

Underline the nouns in the sentences with yellow.

✏️ **Draft Book**

Choose three of the tricky verbs. Write one present tense and one past tense sentence with each verb. Underline the verbs with blue.

Name _____

► In the Backyard

Verbs use tenses to tell when something is happening. When the action will happen in the future, it is future tense. The helping verb *will* is added before the main verb to make it future tense. If the noun is singular, take off the *s* or *es* at the end of the verb before adding *will*.

example: Mom **eats** dinner. (present)
example: Mom **will eat** dinner. (future)

Underline the present tense verb in the first sentence. Add *will* to make the verb future tense in the second sentence.

Dwayne mows the lawn.

Dwayne _____ the lawn.

The crickets chirp.

The crickets _____ .

The chipmunks run into the woods.

The chipmunks _____ into the woods.

Dad plants beans and carrots.

Dad _____ beans and carrots.

🔍 **Review Work**
Underline the nouns in the sentences with yellow.

✏️ **Draft Book**
Write four sentences using verbs in the future tense. Remember to put the helping verb *will* in front of each verb. Underline each verb with blue (including the word *will*).

Name _____

▶ In the Evening

Verbs use tenses to tell when something is happening.

Underline the verbs in the sentences. If the verb is future tense, underline both the main verb and the helping verb *will*. Circle past, present, or future to show the tense.

Aaron's family will play a card game.

past   **present**   **future**

Madeline will sleep all night.

past   **present**   **future**

The children will eat dessert after dinner.

past   **present**   **future**

Dad made dinner.

past   **present**   **future**

Mother makes hot chocolate.

past   **present**   **future**

Ivan reads a book.

past   **present**   **future**

Review Work

Underline the nouns in the sentences with yellow.

Draft Book

Write two sentences for each verb tense. Underline the verbs with blue. Label the sentences past tense, present tense, or future tense.

▶ Rocks and Minerals ▶ linking verbs

Linking verbs are verbs that do not show action. They express a state of being (*to be*). A linking verb connects, or links, two parts of a sentence. Some common linking verbs are *am*, *is*, *are*, and *was*.

example: I **am** left-handed.　　**example:** He **is** an artist.
example: You **are** a gymnast.　　**example:** We **are** best friends.

Underline the linking verbs in the sentences.

I am a rock collector.

My collection is very big.

That rock is black with little gold specks.

That is a pretty rock.

Rocks are fun to collect.

A diamond is a mineral.

Jade is a green mineral.

These are rare minerals.

 Review Work

　Underline the nouns in the sentences with yellow.

 Draft Book

　Write five sentences that use linking verbs.
　Underline the linking verbs with blue.

Name _____

▶ Crawly Creatures   `linking verbs`

Linking verbs are verbs that do not show action. They express a state of being (*to be*). A linking verb connects, or links, two parts of a sentence. The most common linking verbs are *am*, *is*, *are*, and *was*.

Write the correct form of the linking verb in each sentence.

The grasshoppers _____ in the weeds.

A cricket _____ under the deck.

The spider _____ on the web.

The butterfly _____ on the bush.

The ladybugs _____ on the flower stem.

The flies _____ in the air around my head.

The bee _____ in the flower.

The ants _____ in the grass.

I _____ in the grass watching bugs.

🔍 **Review Work**
Underline the nouns in the sentences with yellow.

✏️ **Draft Book**
Write five sentences that use linking verbs.
Underline the linking verbs with blue.

Name _____

Numbers and Colors adjectives

Adjectives are words that describe nouns. Adjectives can tell number or color.

example: Susan ate **two** pieces of candy.
example: The **yellow** pear was in the basket.

Circle the number and color adjectives in the sentences.

Mariella collected twenty fireflies in the jar.

Bev's rabbit ate four carrots.

The brown horses galloped.

Landon gathered sixteen pencils.

Gabe picked the yellow flower.

Ashley only ate the green grapes.

Zelda has a purple headband.

Carlos spent nine dimes.

Many starfish have five legs.

 Review Work

Underline the nouns in the sentences with yellow. Draw an X next to each proper noun.

 Draft Book

Write five sentences. Use color and number adjectives to describe the nouns.

Name _____

▶ Size and Shape
adjectives

Adjectives are words that describe nouns. Adjectives can tell size or shape.
   example: Jillian bought the **square** picture frame.
   example: The **little** boy climbed the rope.

Circle the size and shape adjectives in the sentences.

The circular clock is in the hallway.

Vinny washed the square window.

Carrie bought the thin ribbon.

Look at that small sand castle.

Yuri has an oval skateboard.

Get the dog's long leash.

Terrell caught a tiny fish!

Hannah found her round glasses.

Mae's large bucket is full of sand.

That large spider escaped from its cage!

 Review Work

   Underline the verbs in the sentences with blue.

 Draft Book

   Write five sentences. Use size and shape adjectives to describe
   the nouns.

© Carson-Dellosa

▶ Describers
adjectives

Adjectives are words that describe nouns. Adjectives can tell number, color, size, shape, or anything that adds detail. A sentence can have more than one adjective.

example: **Four** tulips are in my **colorful** garden.

Circle the adjectives in the sentences. Draw an arrow from each adjective to the noun it describes.

Where is the gray bug?

Lenny has hot soup and cold milk for lunch.

Giant dinosaurs lived many years ago.

Eva and Pat used sparkly paint to decorate their pencil boxes.

Selma ate a yellow banana and eleven raisins for snack.

Jessie is singing a beautiful song.

A tired Melina fell asleep on her beach towel.

We went to the county zoo on a sunny day.

Jacob tried to wash and dry his squirming puppy.

🔍 Review Work
Underline the verbs in the sentences with blue.

✏️ Draft Book
Write five sentences that have adjectives in them. Circle the adjectives. Draw an arrow from each adjective to the noun it describes.

▶ More Describers

adjectives

Adjectives are words that describe nouns. Adjectives can tell number, color, size, shape, or anything that adds detail.

Circle the adjectives.

heavy	walked	old	house	loose	book	shoe
twelve	sneezed	dry	star	broken	sing	whale
silly	hairy	blue	school	strong	parked	wrinkled
gold	wiggle	new	awful	friend	tired	blink

Use the adjectives to finish the sentences. Or, write your own adjectives on the lines.

Whitney held that _____ snake.

Jo broke that _____ lamp.

Charlie tried to lift the _____ lamb.

Bailey rode his _____ scooter.

🔍 Review Work

In the word list, underline the nouns with yellow and the verbs with blue.

✏️ Draft Book

Write five sentences that have adjectives in them. Circle the adjectives. Draw an arrow from each adjective to the noun it describes.

Name _____

▶ Mixed-Up Words ▷ nouns, verbs, and adjectives

Sometimes a word that is a noun in one sentence can be a verb or an adjective in another sentence. How the word is used in a sentence determines what type of word it is.

example: That **fly** is bothering me. (noun)
example: I **fly** my kite. (verb)
example: Jamie caught the **fly** ball. (adjective)

What type of word is the underlined word in each sentence? Write noun, verb, or adjective on each line.

I <u>comb</u> the tangles out of my hair. _____

Riley has a red <u>comb</u>. _____

Cassidy likes <u>cherry</u> pie. _____

I want to eat that <u>cherry</u>. _____

The fruit <u>bat</u> hangs upside down to sleep. _____

Juan and Jo <u>bat</u> the ball over the fence. _____

Turn on the <u>light</u>. _____

Gerry carried the <u>light</u> bag. _____

🔍 **Review Work**
Underline the verbs in the sentences with blue.

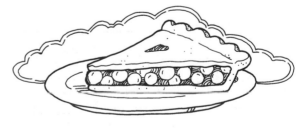

✏️ **Draft Book**
Write two sentences with each of these words: play, watch, paint. Use the words differently in each sentence.

In the Beginning → prefixes *re-* and *un-*

A prefix is a group of letters added to the beginning of a word. The word the prefix is added to is called the root, or base, word. A prefix changes the meaning of the root word. Two common prefixes are *re-* and *un-*. *Re-* means do again. *Un-* means not.

example: reorder = order again   The store will reorder the toy.
example: unsafe = not safe   The park is unsafe at night.

Add *re* to the beginning of each word.

write _____   read _____

wind _____   heat _____

Add *un* to the beginning of each word.

happy _____   known _____

opened _____   zip _____

Use the new words to finish the sentences.

The food is cold. We will have to _____it.

May I have this _____ bag of pretzels?

_____ your jacket and take it off. It is hot!

We need to _____ the videotape.

🔍 **Review Work**
  Underline the verbs in the sentences with blue.

✏️ **Draft Book**
  Write a sentence with each of the four new words not used in the sentences above.

Name _____

▶ At the End

A suffix is a group of letters added to the end of a word. The word the suffix is added to is called the root, or base, word. A suffix changes the meaning of the root word. Two common suffixes are *-er* and *-est*. *-Er* means more. *-Est* means most.

    example: young**er** = more young   Bo is younger than me.
    example: young**est** = most young   Jill is the youngest girl in class.

Add *er* and *est* to the ends of the words.

slow   _____   _____

small   _____   _____

loud   _____   _____

Add *er* or *est* to the end of each word to finish the sentence.

J.J.'s race car is _____ than Joey's.
                       more fast

That is the _____ scarf I've ever felt.
                   most soft

Taylor has the _____ cat in the world!
                   most sweet

Is your sand castle _____ than mine?
                   more tall

🔍 Review Work
Underline the verbs in the sentences with blue.

✎ Draft Book
Write two sentences with each new *-er* and *-est* word.

▶ Tell Me More   adverbs

Adverbs are words that tell more about verbs. They tell how something happens. Usually, adverbs end with *ly*.

Use the adverbs to finish the sentences.

quickly	sadly	slowly	quietly	too	carefully
easily	fast	loudly	softly	well	gracefully

Jenny ran _____ and finished first.

Did Sal ride _____ ?

My friend speaks so _____ I can't hear her.

Will you work _____ ?

Check your homework _____ .

Rianne and Bert danced _____ .

The turtle moved _____ across the yard.

We heard Marlene blow her whistle _____ .

🔍 Review Work

Underline the nouns in the sentences with yellow. Underline the verbs with blue.

✏️ Draft Book

Choose four of the adverbs above and write a sentence with each one. Each adverb should tell how something happened in the sentence.

Name _____

In the Ocean

Adverbs are words that tell more about verbs. They tell how something happens. They also tell where something happens.

Circle the adverbs that tell how in the sentences.

Jade swam peacefully in the ocean.

She saw dolphins jumping gracefully.

Fish were gliding lazily through the water.

Something lightly bumped her leg.

Jade screamed loudly.

Her brother Will quickly turned her around.

"It is just me," he said gently.

Color the seashells that contain adverbs that tell where.

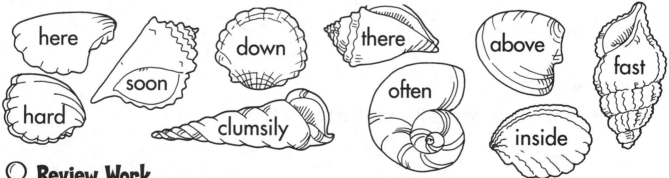

here

soon

hard

down

clumsily

there

often

above

inside

fast

 Review Work

Underline the nouns in the sentences with yellow. Underline the verbs with blue.

 Draft Book

Find a page in your Draft Book with the verbs underlined with blue. Add adverbs to tell where things happened in your sentences.

▶ Now and Then

Adverbs are words that tell more about verbs. They tell how or where something happens. They also tell when something happens.

Circle the adverbs that tell when in the sentences.

Hunter's dog always barks at strangers.

Omar built the doghouse yesterday.

Amie will bring snacks tomorrow.

Lightning had hit the tree before.

Grandma will baby-sit us tonight.

Cleo often studies.

We jumped rope today.

Will Tina do a cartwheel soon?

Brandon calls me daily.

🔍 Review Work

Underline the verbs in the sentences with blue.

✏️ Draft Book

Find a page in your Draft Book with the verbs underlined with blue. Add adverbs to tell when things happened in your sentences. Circle the adverbs with purple.

Name _____

▶ How, Where, or When ▶ adverbs

Adverbs are words that tell more about verbs. They tell how, where, or when something happens.

What does each adverb tell about the verb? Write *how*, *where*, or *when* on each line.

Ben walked **near** the beehive. _____

Rita whispered **quietly** in my ear. _____

Lucy yelled **loudly** at the game. _____

Mrs. Holmes exercises **daily**. _____

Jared arrived at the movie **early**. _____

Adrian's boots are **here**. _____

Darla pedaled her bike **quickly**. _____

Hannah **often** reads books about animals. _____

Drew found the toy **inside** the cereal box. _____

🔍 Review Work

In each sentence, draw an arrow from the adverb to the verb it is telling more about.

✏️ Draft Book

Write a story about a toy you would like to find in a cereal box. Include adverbs. Circle the adverbs with purple.

Name _____

adverbs

Adverbs are words that tell more about verbs. They tell how, where, or when something happens.

Finish each sentence by adding an adverb that tells *how*, *where*, or *when*.

The caterpillar crawled _____ .
                               how

The grasshopper jumped _____ .
                                where

Five ants dragged the crumbs _____ .
                                      when

The dragonfly landed _____ .
                              where

The cricket chirped _____ .
                             how

The butterfly flew _____ the flower.
                            where

🔍 **Review Work**

Underline the verbs in the sentences with blue. Draw an arrow from each adverb to the verb it is telling more about.

✏️ **Draft Book**

Write a story about a garden. Include adverbs. Circle the adverbs with purple.

Name _____

A or An

Articles are small words that come before a noun or an adjective/noun combination.

A and *an* are articles. They signal that one general thing is being talked about. Use *a* if the word after it starts with a consonant sound. Use *an* if the word after it starts with a vowel sound.

Write *a* or *an* before each word or phrase.

_____ dictionary	_____ toy	_____ ocean
_____ deer	_____ beach	_____ ant
_____ egg	_____ lake	_____ ripe orange
_____ house	_____ panda	_____ large slide
_____ icicle	_____ umbrella	_____ elephant
_____ movie	_____ purse	_____ basketball
_____ tennis shoe	_____ tree	_____ igloo
_____ computer	_____ watch	_____ easy problem

Review Work

Write a noun to go with each article.

a _____ an _____

Draft Book

Choose four of the words and write a sentence with each one. Use *a* or *an* in each sentence.

▶ General or Specific? ▶ articles

Articles are small words that come before a noun or an adjective/noun combination.

A, *an*, and *the* are articles. *A* and *an* signal that one general thing is being talked about. Use *a* if the word after it starts with a consonant sound. Use *an* if the word after it starts with a vowel sound. *The* signals that a specific thing is being talked about.

Write *a*, *an*, or *the* on each line.

Skylar made me _____ omelet for breakfast.

I saw _____ woman feeding the birds.

Cory has _____ orange cat.

Can _____ peach roll?

Is _____ oven hot yet?

Diana is _____ best player on the team.

Will you ride in the front seat of _____ car?

Do you live in _____ apartment or _____ house?

🔍 Review Work

Underline the verbs in the sentences with blue. Underline the nouns that come after the articles with yellow.

✏️ Draft Book

Write a story about feeding birds. Use *a*, *an*, or *the* before nouns and adjective/noun combinations. Circle the articles with orange.

▶ Pick the Pronoun ▶ subject pronouns

Pronouns are words that take the place of nouns. A subject pronoun usually comes before a verb. Subject pronouns that take the place of people nouns are *I, you, he, she, we,* and *they*. The pronoun that takes the place of thing nouns is *it*.

Above each group of words, write the pronoun that could replace each word in the group.

_____

school
bike
worm

_____

Martha and George
those shoppers
the first graders

_____

Mom
Mrs. Sosa
Katie

_____

my family and I
my team and I
you and I

Mr. Clark
Jonathan
Grandpa

 Review Work

Add another noun under each group of words.

 Draft Book

Write a story about your family. Use the subject pronouns from this page. Underline the pronouns with red.

Name _____

▶ They Did It

Pronouns are words that take the place of nouns. A subject pronoun usually comes before a verb. Subject pronouns that take the place of people nouns are *I, you, he, she, we,* and *they.* The pronoun that takes the place of a singular thing noun is *it.*

Which pronoun could replace the bold word(s) in each sentence? Write the correct pronoun on the line.

My mom delivered cupcakes to our classroom. _____

Sally paid for lunch. _____

Hailey and Dan built a huge fort. _____

The wind blew over the swing set. _____

Iris and I crawled through the tunnel. _____

Joshua cleaned Mom's fishbowl. _____

Dave's horses galloped across the pasture. _____

Delaney's grandparents arrived at noon. _____

Dad golfed on Saturday. _____

🔍 **Review Work**

Underline the verbs in the sentences with blue.

✏️ **Draft Book**

Write a story about building a fort. Use the subject pronouns from this page. Underline the pronouns with red.

© Carson-Dellosa

Name _____

 # After the Verb   **object pronouns**

Pronouns are words that take the place of nouns. An object pronoun usually comes after a verb. Object pronouns are *me, you, him, her, us, them,* and *it.*

Which pronoun could replace the bold word(s) in each sentence? Write the correct pronoun on the line.

Jessica fixed **the necklace**. _____

Zachary hit the baseball to **Steve**. _____

The pilot flew **Jessica** to California. _____

Alex pushed **Danielle and me** on the swings. _____

Aunt Lynn took **Meg and Beth** to the zoo. _____

I handed the paper to **Mrs. Willis**. _____

Erik painted **the mural**. _____

Matt sent **Anne** a letter. _____

Stefanie played a game with **Jeremy and Spencer**. _____

Review Work

Underline the nouns in the sentences that could be changed to subject pronouns. Choose four of those nouns and write the correct pronoun above each one.

Draft Book

Write a story about going to the zoo. Use the object pronouns from this page. Underline the pronouns with red.

► Find the Nouns

pronouns

Pronouns are words that take the place of nouns.

A pronoun is bold in the second sentence of each set. Circle the noun and/or pronoun in the first sentence that the pronoun replaces.

Stan has a rabbit. **He** has a brown and white rabbit.

Carl and I are friends. **We** have been friends for a long time.

I like cookies. I like **them** with milk.

Tina has a bike. **She** has a red bike.

I gave the book to Leo. I gave it to **him**.

Teresa has a fishbowl. Teresa has a turtle in **it**.

Liz made lunch for Olga and Yasmine. Liz made sandwiches for **them**.

Mr. Evans drove Tim and me to school. Mr. Evans drove **us** to school.

🔍 Review Work

Underline the verbs in the sentences with blue.

✏️ Draft Book

Write a story about a pet you have or would like to have. Use subject and object pronouns. Underline the pronouns with red.

Name _____

Pronouns are words that take the place of nouns. *I* is a pronoun. It is the word you use when you talk about yourself. Like proper nouns, the word *I* is always capitalized.

Complete the postcard by writing the letter *i* in the blanks. Capitalize *i* if it stands alone as a word, if it is the first letter of someone's name, or if it is the first letter of a word at the beginning of a sentence.

Dear _____sabel,

_____ went to the zoo. The

l_____on roared when he saw

me. _____ was scared. _____t

was fun. _____ hope to see you

on Fr_____day.

        S_____ncerely,

        J_____mmy _____cko

M_____ss _____sabel D_____llon

12 Woodward Dr_____ve

Th_____stown Oregon 12345

 Review Work

Underline the proper nouns on the postcard with yellow. Place a comma between the city and state in the address.

Draft Book

Write a short note to a friend. Remember to capitalize the letter *i* when needed.

Name _____

▶ Sleepover

Pronouns are words that take the place of nouns. *I* is a pronoun. It is the word you use when you talk about yourself. Like proper nouns, the word *I* is always capitalized.

Complete the postcard by writing the letter *i* in the blanks. Capitalize *i* if it stands alone as a word, if it is the first letter of someone's name, or if it is the first letter of a word at the beginning of a sentence.

Dear Ol _____ver,

_____ can't wa_____t unt_____l you come over. _____t w_____ll be my f_____rst sleepover.

_____ have lots of games planned for us. _____ th_____nk we w_____ll stay up all n_____ght!

      Your fr_____end,

      W_____ll _____rstman

Ol_____ver L_____n

284 _____rw_____n Avenue

_____ngles_____de Nebraska

68901

🔍 Review Work

Draw a triangle above each proper noun on the postcard that names a place. Draw an X next to each proper noun that names a person. Place a comma between the city and state in the address.

✏️ Draft Book

Write a short note to your mom or dad. Remember to capitalize the letter *i* when needed.

Name _____

▶ Tiny or Small?

Words that mean about the same thing are called synonyms.
example: **Quick**, **swift**, and **speedy** mean the same thing as **fast**.
example: **Beautiful**, **attractive**, and **lovely** mean the same thing as **pretty**.

The synonyms for *big*, *happy*, *little*, and *cold* are mixed up.
Write the correct synonyms for each word on the lines.

large	glad
tiny	icy
chilly	small
huge	cheerful

big   _____   _____

happy   _____   _____

little _____   _____

cold   _____   _____

 Review Work

Use one of the synonyms for *big* in a sentence.

_____

Use one of the synonyms for *happy* in a sentence.

_____

 Draft Book

Write a story about going to the beach. Use a variety of synonyms to make the story interesting.

CD-4337 Grammar Rules! Grades 1–2   **67**

Name _____

▶ The Same Stuff

Words that mean about the same thing are called synonyms.

Write a synonym from the list for each bold word.

buddies	choose	close	enjoys
fantastic	purchase	race	scream

Lonnie **likes** ice cream. _____

Please **shut** the door to the ferret cage. _____

Eva and Marge will **run** to the swings. _____

Jason will **pick** which book to read. _____

I need to **buy** new crayons. _____

That is a **great** painting! _____

Did you **yell** when you saw the spider? _____

Jeanie and Joan are my best **friends**. _____

🔍 **Review Work**

Underline the nouns in the sentences with yellow.

✏️ **Draft Book**

Write a story about playing outside during recess. Use a variety of synonyms from this page to make the story interesting.

▶ Opposites
antonyms

Words that mean the opposite of each other are called antonyms.

example: The opposite of **fast** is **slow**.

example: The opposite of **nice** is **mean**.

Circle the word in each group that is the antonym of the first word.

hot	little	cold	summer	**wet**	soft	thirsty	dry
long	short	red	heavy	**asleep**	tired	awake	reading
cheerful	full	sad	happy	**stand**	eat	drink	sit
on	slow	off	heavy	**tall**	short	funny	loud
easy	yell	hard	blue	**dirty**	smooth	melted	clean

 Review Work

Choose a pair of antonyms. Write a sentence using both words.

_____

_____

✏ **Draft Book**

Write a story about summer vacation. Use a variety of antonyms and other words from this page to make the story interesting.

▶ Change the Meaning ▶ antonyms

Words that mean the opposite of each other are called antonyms. When a word is replaced by its antonym in a sentence, the meaning of the sentence changes.

example: The pie is **hot**.
example: The pie is **cold**.

Use the words to write an antonym for each bold word.

first	clean	large	hate
quiet	heavy	inside	short

Carlos and I like **loud** music. _____

We played **outside** last night. _____

Grace will eat a **small** snack before the game. _____

Julie, Fred, and Willa **love** chocolate. _____

That movie about Alaska was very **long**. _____

Our **last** day of school will be June 8. _____

This box of red apples is very **light**. _____

After playing outside, Logan was **dirty**. _____

 Review Work

    Underline the verbs in the sentences with blue. Next to each sentence, write the verb tense: P = present, S = past, or F = future.

✎ **Draft Book**

    Choose a new pair of antonyms. Write a sentence using both words.

Name _____

▶ Sounds the Same ▶ homophones

Homophones are words that sound alike but are spelled differently and have different meanings.

Draw lines to match the homophones.

blue

sail

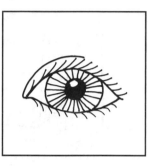
eye

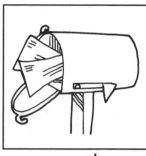
mail

sale

male

blew

I

 Review Work

Write the homophone for each word.

son _____   eight _____

 Draft Book

Choose one pair of homophones. Write a sentence using both words.

_____

_____

Name _____

Homophones are words that sound alike but are spelled differently and have different meanings.

Draw lines to match the homophones.

bear

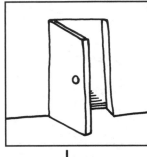
close

heal

berry

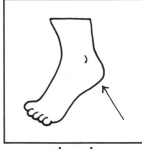
heel

clothes

bury

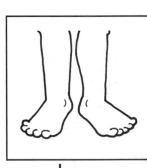
bare

 Review Work

Write the homophone for each word.

meat _____   week _____

 Draft Book

Choose one pair of homophones. Write a sentence using both words.

_____

_____

Name _____

Pear or Pair?

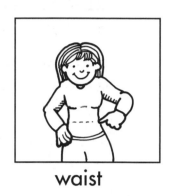homophones

Homophones are words that sound alike but are spelled differently and have different meanings.

Draw lines to match the homophones.

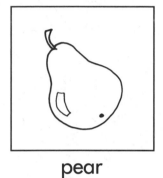
pear

flour

one

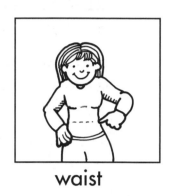
waist

flower

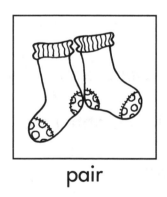
pair

waste

won

 Review Work

Write the homophone for each word.

deer _____   plain _____

Draft Book

Choose one pair of homophones. Write a sentence using both words.

_____

_____

To, Too, Two

homophones

Homophones are words that sound alike but are spelled differently and have different meanings. *To*, *too*, and *two* are homophones.

To is used to show direction or purpose.
example: Nell went **to** school.
example: She likes **to** sing.

Too means also or more than enough.
example: Zander wants some milk, **too**.
example: That popcorn has **too** much salt on it!

Two is the number word for the numeral 2.
example: Ramone has **two** sisters.

Write *to*, *too*, or *two* to finish each sentence.

Are you checking out _____ books?

Is your birthday on January 1, _____ ?

Jackie is going _____ the ballet program tonight.

The muffins are _____ hot to eat right now.

Please hand those _____ papers _____ Andrew.

I am riding my bike _____ the park, _____ .

That shirt was _____ small, so I gave it _____ Paula.

🔍 **Review Work**

Underline the verbs in the sentences with blue. Circle each form of the linking verb *to be*.

✏️ **Draft Book**

Write one sentence each with *to*, *too*, and *two*.

▶ I Hear You!

Homophones are words that sound alike but are spelled differently and have different meanings. *Here/hear* and *by/buy* are homophones.

example: I am sitting right **here**.

example: I **hear** the radio.

example: Put the flowers **by** the window.

example: Will you **buy** peanuts at the circus?

Write *here, hear, by,* or *buy* to finish each sentence.

Can you _____ the screams of the people on the roller coaster?

Put the bananas right _____ on the table.

_____ a movie ticket for me, too.

Bart said he could _____ the water dripping.

Ryan is standing _____ the flagpole.

That book was written _____ Dr. Seuss.

Put the book _____ and the paper there.

Please _____ milk and bread at the store.

🔍 **Review Work**

Circle the articles in the sentences with orange.

✏️ **Draft Book**

Write one sentence each with *here, hear, by,* and *buy*.

▶ They're Over There ▷ homophones

Homophones are words that sound alike but are spelled differently and have different meanings. *There*, *their*, and *they're* are homophones.

There is a place word.　　　　**example:** Sit over **there**.

Their is a belonging word.　　**example:** Shelby is **their** dog.

They're is a contraction for　　**example:** **They're** playing outside.
they are.

Write *there*, *their*, or *they're* to finish each sentence.

The long, strong, slithery pythons are over _____ .

_____ going to see the huge elephants, snakes, and bears.

The two large, feathered eagles wanted _____ dinner.

_____ planning to find the tropical toucans with the colorful, curved beaks.

_____ are the funny chimpanzees, gorillas, and orangutans!

The talented chimpanzees can hold, peel, and eat _____ green bananas.

The zookeeper said that _____ owls, bats, and foxes are in the nocturnal house, which is over _____ .

🔍 **Review Work**

Circle the adjectives in the sentences. Draw an arrow from each adjective to the noun it describes.

✏️ **Draft Book**

Write one sentence each with *there*, *their*, and *they're*.

Name _____

▶ No, I Don't Know ▶ homophones

Homophones are words that sound alike but are spelled differently and have different meanings. *No/know* and *write/right* are homophones.

No is the antonym of yes.
example: **No**, you can't do that!

Know is a verb that means to understand.
example: I **know** how to read.

Write is a verb that means to communicate through letters.
example: I can **write** my name.

Right means correct or the opposite of left.
example: That answer is **right**.
example: Hold up your **right** hand.

Write *no, know, write,* or *right* to finish each sentence.

Do you _____ if it is snowing in Ohio?

Great job, that answer is _____ !

Turn _____ at the corner by Oak Lane.

Rob will _____ his name at the top of the page.

Is yes or _____ the _____ answer?

I _____ that we will _____ stories on Monday.

⌕ Review Work

Draw an X next to each proper noun that names a person. Draw a triangle above each proper noun that names a place.

✏ Draft Book

Write one sentence each with *no, know, write,* and *right*.

Name _____

▶ Get Together

Sometimes two words can be put together to make a new word with its own meaning. This new word is called a compound word.

example: farm + house = farmhouse

Write each word pair as a compound word.

sun + light = _____

birth + day = _____

every + one = _____

rain + bow = _____

water + melon = _____

bare + foot = _____

home + work = _____

mid + night = _____

rail + road = _____

🔍 Review Work

Choose two compound words. Write a sentence with each word.

_____

_____

✏️ Draft Book

Write a story about going to a birthday party. Include as many compound words as you can.

Name _____

One and One Is Two > compound words

Sometimes two words can be put together to make a new word with its own meaning. This new word is called a compound word.

Write each word pair as a compound word.

after + noon = _____

back + yard = _____

class + mate = _____

break + fast = _____

flash + light = _____

oat + meal = _____

pop + corn = _____

Use the compound words to finish the sentences.

Nate saw fireflies in his _____ .

Ricky will need a _____ when he camps outside.

Claire likes to eat _____ at the movies.

 Review Work

Underline the other compound words in the sentences.

 Draft Book

Write a sentence with each compound word that was not used in one of the sentences above.

Name _____

▶ **I Will Not**

A contraction is two words that are put together to make one word. Some of the letters drop out of the second word when the words are joined. An apostrophe takes the place of the dropped letters.

    example: did + not = didn't

Draw lines to match the word pairs with their contractions.

are not	couldn't
were not	isn't
could not	aren't
did not	haven't
do not	wasn't
have not	don't
is not	didn't
was not	weren't

Write a contraction on the line to finish each sentence.

We **are not** _____ going to the circus tonight.

Gerard **did not** _____ play basketball today.

It **is not** _____ raining outside now.

You **do not** _____ need a jacket.

🔍 **Review Work**

    Circle the adverbs that tell when with purple.

✏️ **Draft Book**

    Choose five contractions. Write a sentence with each one.

Name _____

▶ Yes, We Will

A contraction is two words that are put together to make one word. Some of the letters drop out of the second word when the words are joined. An apostrophe takes the place of the dropped letters.

The verb *will* can be combined with pronouns to make contractions.

example: I + will = I'll   **example:** he + will = he'll

Write the word pair for each contraction.

we'll _____   she'll _____

they'll _____   you'll _____

Write a contraction on the line to finish each sentence.

I will _____ bring in my photo album on Thursday.

My parents decided that **we will** _____ leave for Niagara Falls tomorrow.

I think **you will** _____ be able to do at least 20 sit-ups.

Maria's friends think **they will** _____ go to see the fireworks.

Theo said **he will** _____ play his tuba this afternoon.

 **Review Work**

Underline the nouns in the sentences with yellow. Draw an X next to each proper noun that names a person. Draw a triangle above each proper noun that names a place.

Draft Book

Write a sentence with each contraction on this page.

Name _____

 **Won't**

A contraction is two words that are put together to make one word. Some of the letters drop out of the second word when the words are joined. An apostrophe takes the place of the dropped letters.

The verb *will* can be combined with the word *not* to make *won't*.

Underline the contraction in each sentence. Rewrite each sentence by changing the contraction to the pronoun and adding *won't*. The first one has been done for you.

<u>We'll</u> go swimming today.

We won't go swimming today.

_____

Fiona said she'll order apple pie.

_____

Next year, he'll be in fourth grade.

_____

You'll need to help shovel the snow.

_____

They'll clear the table and do the dishes.

_____

 Review Work

What two words make up the contraction *won't*?

_____   _____

 Draft Book

Write a story about washing the dishes. Use the contraction *won't*.

Name _____

Put Them Together > contractions

A contraction is two words that are put together to make one word. Some of the letters drop out of the second word when the words are joined. An apostrophe takes the place of the dropped letters.

Draw lines to match the word pairs with their contractions.

he is	she's
I would	he'd
she is	they've
you have	I'm
we are	let's
he would	I've
they have	he's
they are	you're
I am	what's
what is	you've
you are	I'd
I have	they're
let us	we're

 Review Work

Circle each form of the linking verb *to be*.

 Draft Book

Write a sentence with each contraction on this page.

CD-4337 Grammar Rules! Grades 1–2 **83**

▶ Think About It

A contraction is two words that are put together to make one word. Some of the letters usually drop out of the second word when the words are joined. An apostrophe takes the place of the dropped letters.

Write a contraction on the line to finish the sentence.

Jill _____ climb that enormous tree.
will not

The sign says _____ need a green ticket to get in.
you will

I think _____ eating a hot dinner soon.
we are

_____ the recipe for bread dough?
What is

That _____ the fourth bell.
was not

_____ ridden the yellow bus to school.
She had

_____ feeding the two hamsters this week?
Who is

🔍 **Review Work**

Circle the adjectives in the sentences. Draw an arrow from each adjective to the noun it describes.

✏️ **Draft Book**

Write a story about climbing a tree. Use contractions in your story.

▶ Beginning Letters ▷ sentences

A sentence is a group of words that tells a complete thought. A sentence always starts with an uppercase letter.

Rewrite the sentences. Start each sentence with an uppercase letter. Circle the uppercase letter at the beginning of each sentence.

i like studying grammar.

_____

mary will underline nouns with yellow.

_____

sandy and Kit underline verbs with blue.

_____

janice circled the first noun in the sentence.

_____

 Review Work

Underline the verbs in the sentences with blue. Next to each sentence, write the verb tense: P = present, S = past, or F = future.

 Draft Book

Write four sentences about reading your favorite book. Start each sentence with an uppercase letter. Circle the uppercase letter at the beginning of each sentence.

Name _____

▶ One Day

A sentence is a group of words that tells a complete thought. A sentence always starts with an uppercase letter.

Circle the first letter of each sentence. Write an uppercase letter next to each lowercase letter that needs to be changed.

in the afternoon, we learn about science.

i get to school at 8:45 A.M.

i sit down at my desk.

olivia helps with the calendar.

my pencil breaks during math.

miss Acker reads a great book.

the class eats lunch.

we clean out our messy desks.

ryan picks me up after school.

miss Acker will teach us about volcanoes tomorrow.

🔍 Review Work

Underline the verbs in the sentences with blue. Write an *F* next to the sentence that is written in future tense.

✏️ Draft Book

Write three sentences about your favorite season. Start each sentence with an uppercase letter. Circle the uppercase letter at the beginning of each sentence.

Star or X

A sentence is a group of words that tells a complete thought. A sentence always starts with an uppercase letter and ends with a punctuation mark.

example: Janice has a dog. (sentence)

example: A dog. (not a sentence)

If the group of words is a sentence, draw a star in the box. If it is not a sentence, draw an X in the box.

☐ April tossed the ball to Latrell.

☐ Grapes are Lamar's favorite snack.

☐ The scary movie.

☐ Oranges, apples, and bananas.

☐ Dragonflies eat mosquitoes.

☐ Making noise.

☐ The watermelon is juicy.

☐ Andra's baseball bat.

☐ In the spider web.

Review Work

Underline the verbs with blue. Underline the nouns with yellow.

Draft Book

Choose three groups of words from above that are not sentences. Add your own words to each to make three complete sentences.

Name _____

▶ Find the Stars

A sentence is a group of words that tells a complete thought. A sentence always starts with an uppercase letter and ends with a punctuation mark.

example: Is that Quincy's fish? (sentence)
example: Is that? (not a sentence)

If the group of words is a sentence, draw a star in the box. If it is not a sentence, draw an X in the box.

☐ When will Ross call me?

☐ Write it?

☐ Is Helene?

☐ Will you climb the ladder?

☐ Where is the bird going?

☐ In the cave?

☐ What kind of juice do you like?

☐ Who can help me open the jar?

☐ Will the?

 Review Work
Underline the pronouns with red.

Draft Book
Choose three groups of words from above that are not sentences. Add your own words to each to make three complete sentences.

Make the Fix

sentences

A sentence is a group of words that tells a complete thought. A sentence always starts with an uppercase letter and ends with a punctuation mark.

Add words to make each group of words a complete sentence. Start each sentence with an uppercase letter and put the correct punctuation mark at the end.

runs to

_____

will Dean

_____

get a

_____

the brown cow

_____

begins at noon

_____

 Review Work

Circle the adjectives in the sentences you wrote. Draw an arrow from each adjective to the noun it describes.

Draft Book

Find a full page of writing in your Draft Book. Circle the punctuation marks.

 # Snow Day

statements

There are four types of sentences. A telling, or declarative, sentence tells something. A declarative sentence can also be called a statement. A declarative sentence always ends with a period.

Rewrite the declarative sentences. Start each sentence with an uppercase letter and put a period at the end.

snowmen melt in the sun

_____

mittens keep her hands warm

_____

julian packs snow into snowballs

_____

zoe makes tunnels in the snowbank

_____

travis and Stephen build an igloo

_____

 Review Work
Underline the nouns in the sentences with yellow.

Draft Book
Write four declarative sentences about playing in the snow. Start each sentence with an uppercase letter. End each sentence with a period.

▶ That Does It   statements

There are four types of sentences. A telling, or declarative, sentence tells something. A declarative sentence can also be called a statement. A declarative sentence always ends with a period.

Use the words to finish the declarative sentences. End each sentence with a period.

bread   letters   marshmallows   music
stories   teeth   pictures   time

A piano makes _____

An oven bakes _____

Your brother reads you _____

A dentist takes care of _____

The clock tells _____

I like writing _____

That fire roasts _____

A crayon colors _____

🔍 Review Work

Circle the uppercase letter at the beginning of each sentence. Circle the period at the end of each sentence.

✏️ Draft Book

Write three declarative sentences about roasting marshmallows. Start each sentence with an uppercase letter. End each sentence with a period.

▶ I Want to Know ▶ questions

There are four types of sentences. An asking, or interrogative, sentence asks a question. An interrogative sentence can also be called a question. An interrogative sentence always ends with a question mark.

Rewrite the interrogative sentences. Start each sentence with an uppercase letter and put a question mark at the end.

who got the book

_____

where is my friend

_____

what is that bug called

_____

why are you laughing

_____

when are we leaving

_____

🔍 **Review Work**

In the sentences, circle each form of the linking verb *to be*.

✏️ **Draft Book**

Write four interrogative sentences about going to lunch. Start each sentence with an uppercase letter. End each sentence with a question mark.

Name _____

There are four types of sentences. An asking, or interrogative, sentence asks a question. An interrogative sentence can also be called a question. An interrogative sentence always ends with a question mark.

Use the words to finish the interrogative sentences. End each sentence with a question mark.

crayons	bag	desk	sneeze
lunch	fit	dot	sticky

Is the glue _____

Do elephants _____

Do your new shoes _____

Is an ant as small as a _____

What will you eat for _____

Will you color with the _____

Why are you sitting at my _____

What is in your_____

 Review Work

Circle the uppercase letter at the beginning of each sentence. Circle the question mark at the end of each sentence.

 Draft Book

Write three interrogative sentences about elephants. Start each sentence with an uppercase letter. End each sentence with a question mark.

▶ Put an End to It

statements and questions

A declarative sentence tells something and ends with a period. An interrogative sentence asks a question and ends with a question mark. A period and a question mark are called punctuation marks.

Write the correct punctuation mark at the end of each sentence.

Where is my pencil ☐

Geoffrey likes to use his computer ☐

Penguins live in Antarctica ☐

Who can help me tie my shoe ☐

What color is your bike ☐

When is Miguel coming over ☐

Carrots are good to eat ☐

My family likes to go to the museum ☐

Will you help me find my soccer ball ☐

🔍 **Review Work**

Underline the verbs in the sentences with blue.

✏️ **Draft Book**

Write two interrogative sentences and two declarative sentences about penguins. Start each sentence with an uppercase letter. End each sentence with the correct punctuation mark.

Name _____

A declarative sentence tells something and ends with a period. An interrogative sentence asks a question and ends with a question mark. A period and a question mark are called punctuation marks.

Write the correct punctuation mark at the end of each sentence.

A tree grows in our backyard ☐

Are the leaves on the branches important to the tree ☐

The leaves make food for the tree ☐

Leaves also store food ☐

What do the roots do ☐

The roots pull in water and minerals ☐

Where do seeds come from ☐

Seeds form in the seed pods ☐

Do trees have flowers ☐

Trees have flowers or cones ☐

 Review Work
   Underline the nouns in the sentences with yellow.

 Draft Book
   Write three interrogative sentences and three declarative sentences about trees. Start each sentence with an uppercase letter. End each sentence with the correct punctuation mark.

Where Are They?

A declarative sentence tells something and ends with a period. An interrogative sentence asks a question and ends with a question mark. A period and a question mark are called punctuation marks.

Write the correct punctuation mark at the end of each sentence.

Where do monarch butterflies come from ☐

Monarch butterflies are from Mexico ☐

Where do dolphins live ☐

Dolphins live in the ocean ☐

Where do elephants live ☐

Elephants are from Asia and Africa ☐

Where can spiders be found ☐

Spiders live nearly everywhere on Earth ☐

Review Work

Underline the nouns in the sentences with yellow. Draw a triangle above each proper noun that names a place.

Draft Book

Choose a topic and write three interrogative sentences and three declarative sentences about it. Start each sentence with an uppercase letter. End each sentence with the correct punctuation mark.

Name _____

A declarative sentence tells something and ends with a period. An interrogative sentence asks a question and ends with a question mark. A period and a question mark are called punctuation marks.

Look at each answer and write a question that could be asked. Start each question with an uppercase letter and end with a question mark. The first one has been done for you.

Question: What does four plus five equal?

Answer: Four plus five equals nine.

Question: _____

Answer: Yes, I have my pencil right here.

Question: _____

Answer: It is 11:30 A.M.

Question: _____

Answer: An interrogative sentence is a sentence that asks a question.

Question: _____

Answer: Yes, we are ready to go to lunch.

🔍 Review Work

Circle the first letter of each sentence. Circle the ending punctuation marks. Draw a star next to each interrogative sentence.

 Draft Book

Choose a topic and write your own set of interrogative and declarative sentences. Start each sentence with an uppercase letter. End each sentence with the correct punctuation mark.

Name _____

 **Wow!**

There are four types of sentences. An exclamatory sentence is used when the writer wants to show strong feelings. An exclamatory sentence always ends with an exclamation mark.

Rewrite the exclamatory sentences. Start each sentence with an uppercase letter and put an exclamation mark at the end.

i did not break that window

_____

this is the best gift I've ever gotten

_____

i see a shooting star

_____

ouch, that really hurt

_____

 Review Work

Choose one sentence. Draw a check mark next to it. If that sentence was an answer, write a follow-up question.

_____

Draft Book

Write four exclamatory sentences about the best gift you've ever received. Start each sentence with an uppercase letter. End each sentence with an exclamation mark.

▶ Great!  exclamations

There are four types of sentences. An exclamatory sentence is used when the writer wants to show strong feelings. An exclamatory sentence always ends with an exclamation mark.

Use the words to finish the exclamatory sentences. End each sentence with an exclamation mark.

good   foot   test   beach
building   snake   glass   school

This pie tastes _____

We are going to the _____

That _____ scared me

I did not break that _____

That _____ is tall

Don't step on my _____

I passed the _____

I can't wait for _____ to start

🔍 **Review Work**

Circle the uppercase letter at the beginning of each sentence. Circle the exclamation mark at the end of each sentence.

✏️ **Draft Book**

Write three exclamatory sentences. Start each sentence with an uppercase letter. End each sentence with an exclamation mark.

▶ Now Do This

There are four types of sentences. An imperative sentence tells you what to do or makes a request. An imperative sentence can also be called a command. An imperative sentence usually ends with a period.

Rewrite the imperative sentences. Start each sentence with an uppercase letter and put a period at the end.

clean your room

_____

stop tickling me

_____

take the dog for a walk before dinner

_____

wait until the bell rings before you leave

_____

turn off the television

_____

🔍 **Review Work**

Underline the verbs in the sentences with blue.

✏️ **Draft Book**

Choose a topic and write five imperative sentences. Start each sentence with an uppercase letter. End each sentence with a period.

Name _____

Together Again

There are four types of sentences. An imperative sentence tells you what to do or makes a request. An imperative sentence can also be called a command. An imperative sentence usually ends with a period.

Match the two halves of each command. Write the sentences correctly. Start each sentence with an uppercase letter and end with a period.

use a crayon	to eat that candy
wait until later	before it stops ringing
answer the phone	to color the picture
take the ice	on this paper
write the story	out of the freezer

_____

_____

_____

_____

_____

 Review Work

Underline the imperative sentences in the directions.

 Draft Book

Write five imperative sentences. Start each sentence with an uppercase letter. End each sentence with a period.

Name _____

A sentence is a group of words that tells a complete thought. A sentence always starts with an uppercase letter and ends with a punctuation mark.

Cross out the first letter in each sentence and write the uppercase letter next to it. Circle the correct punctuation mark at the end.

_____ does Angie know how to read   .   !   ?

_____ emory baked a chocolate cake   .   !   ?

_____ justin turned on the computer   .   !   ?

_____ eat your lunch   .   !   ?

_____ the snake is loose   .   !   ?

_____ turn off the light   .   !   ?

_____ when will the parade start   .   !   ?

_____ help, my hand is stuck   .   !   ?

🔍 **Review Work**

Count how many of each type of sentence are shown.

declarative: _____   interrogative: _____

exclamatory: _____   imperative: _____

✏️ **Draft Book**

Find a full page of writing in your Draft Book. Circle the punctuation marks. If a punctuation mark is not correct, fix it.

Name _____

▶ What Type?

A sentence is a group of words that tells a complete thought. A sentence always starts with an uppercase letter and ends with a punctuation mark.

Cross out the first letter in each sentence and write the uppercase letter next to it. Circle the correct punctuation mark at the end.

_____ tommy laughed at the clown . ! ?

_____ clean your room . ! ?

_____ does Donna have a hole in her shoe . ! ?

_____ there is a mouse in the kitchen . ! ?

_____ ray painted a picture . ! ?

_____ what is your favorite color . ! ?

_____ go to bed . ! ?

_____ do you want to play . ! ?

🔍 Review Work

Underline the nouns in the sentences with yellow. Draw an X next to each proper noun. Underline the verbs in the sentences with blue.

✏️ Draft Book

Write two sentences of each type. Label them. Start each sentence with an uppercase letter. End each sentence with the correct punctuation mark.

▶ The Right Ending

sentence types

There are four types of sentences.
1 - declarative: tells something, ends with a period
2 - interrogative: asks a question, ends with a question mark
3 - exclamatory: shows strong feelings, ends with an exclamation point
4 - imperative: gives a command or request, usually ends with a period

Decide which type each sentence is. Write the number in the box before the sentence. Write the correct punctuation mark in the box after the sentence.

☐ What time are we going to the pool ☐

☐ Finish your work ☐

☐ How far is Nevada from Iowa ☐

☐ Why do worms eat dirt ☐

☐ Lebron has a bunk bed ☐

☐ Wow, that idea is fantastic ☐

☐ Get the map ☐

☐ I like spaghetti ☐

🔍 **Review Work**

Underline the nouns in the sentences with yellow.

✏️ **Draft Book**

Write two sentences of each type. Label them. Start each sentence with an uppercase letter. End each sentence with the correct punctuation mark.

Name _____

There are four types of sentences.
1 - declarative: tells something, ends with a period
2 - interrogative: asks a question, ends with a question mark
3 - exclamatory: shows strong feelings, ends with an exclamation point
4 - imperative: gives a command or request, usually ends with a period

Decide which type each sentence is. Write the number in the box before the sentence. Write the correct punctuation mark in the box after the sentence.

☐ Keisha's bike needs to be washed ☐

☐ That ball is heading for Neil's head ☐

☐ Take Frank's paper out of the trash ☐

☐ Yuck, Xavier's knee is bleeding ☐

☐ Where are Emma's mittens ☐

☐ Hal is reading Eliza's story ☐

☐ What time does Ally's recital start ☐

☐ Hector's fish is orange with black spots ☐

🔍 **Review Work**

Underline the possessive nouns in the sentences with yellow.

✏️ **Draft Book**

Write three sentences of each type. Label them. Start each sentence with an uppercase letter. End each sentence with the correct punctuation mark.

Name _____

▶ Separate Them

 commas

A comma is a type of punctuation mark used to separate a group of three or more words in a list or series.

example: Sal ate **grapes**, **yogurt**, and **soup** for lunch.

Put commas between the words in each series.

Tim went fishing on Wednesday Friday Saturday and Monday.

Ahmad Spencer Reese and Jeremy played soccer.

Garrett Faith Justin and I drove to the festival.

The fair had rides food animals and games.

George likes to play with Zack Tommy Cole and me.

Antoine's favorite subjects are math reading and science.

Perry has relatives in Florida Indiana and Tennessee.

 Review Work

In the sentences, draw an X next to each proper noun that names a person. Write the correct pronoun above each noun. If the nouns are separated by commas, write the pronoun that describes the entire group.

Draft Book

Write four sentences each with a list of three or more words. Put commas between the words in each list.

Name _____

▶ What Type of Word? ▶ commas

A comma is a type of punctuation mark used to separate a group of three or more words in a list or series.

> **example:** **Austin**, **Javier**, and **Owen** went hiking. (nouns)
> **example:** Mia can **run**, **hop**, and **jump**. (verbs)
> **example:** Throw that **skinny**, **little**, **broken** crayon away. (adjectives)
> **example:** Rabbits hopped **over**, **under**, and **between** the plants. (adverbs)

Circle the commas in the sentences. Write what type of words (noun, verb, adjective, or adverb) the commas separate in each sentence.

Tyesha walked quickly, quietly, and carefully away from the beehive.

_____

Molly bikes, hikes, and swims when she goes camping.

_____

We saw anteaters, zebras, jaguars, and bats at the zoo.

_____

I like fresh, hot, salty, buttery popcorn.

_____

⌕ Review Work

Underline the pronouns in the sentences with red.

 Draft Book

Write four sentences each with a list of three or more words. Put commas between the words in each list.

▶ How Many?

A comma is a type of punctuation mark used to separate a group of three or more words in a list or series.

Circle the commas in the sentences. Answer the questions.

We bought bananas, cherry tomatoes, beans, and onions at the market.

How many things did we buy? _____

Lynda, Myong, and Joanne made beaded bracelets.

How many girls made beaded bracelets? _____

Brady walked, hopped, crawled, and skipped through the obstacle course.

How many things did Brady do? _____

Richard saw starfish, eels, clams, fish, and spiny lobsters at the aquarium.

How many types of things did Richard see? _____

Pack your toothbrush, sleeping bag, pillow, and pajamas.

How many things should you pack? _____

🔍 **Review Work**

Circle the adjectives in the sentences. Draw an arrow from each adjective to the noun it describes.

✏️ **Draft Book**

Write four sentences each with a list of three or more words. Put commas between the words in each list.

Commas in Dates

commas

A comma is a type of punctuation mark used to separate a group of three or more words in a list or series. Commas are also used in certain dates to separate the day of the week, the month and date, and the year.

example: Monday, August 11
example: Monday, August 11, 2003
example: August 11, 2003

Some dates don't need commas.
example: August 11   **example:** August 2003

Put commas where they are needed in the dates. Write an uppercase letter above each lowercase letter that needs to be changed.

tuesday november 12 1996   thursday march 20

december 30 2004   july 1885

wednesday april 24 2002   september 4 1984

dustin's birthday is january 21.

nina started second grade on august 27 1999.

karen will graduate in june 2010.

ian was born on monday august 26 1991.

 Review Work

Choose one sentence. Rewrite it as a question.

_____

 Draft Book

Write three sentences with dates. Put commas where they are needed.

Name _____

▶ Dinnertime

Quotation marks are a type of punctuation mark used to go around the words that people say.

    example: "You did a great job!" said Bruce.

Put quotation marks around the words that people are saying in the sentences.

May I have some chips? asked Liv.

Mom replied, No, we're going to eat dinner soon.

How about some grapes? questioned Darian.

How about helping me finish dinner? suggested Mom.

Can I get a vegetable plate ready? I can do that! exclaimed Liv.

Mom smiled. That would be a big help, Liv.

I'll set the table, said Darian.

Thanks! Dinner is almost ready, said Mom.

All done, said Darian.

Me, too! shouted Liv.

 Review Work

    In the sentences, underline the verbs that are used in place of the verb *said*.

 Draft Book

    Write a story about a conversation you had with a friend or family member. Put quotation marks around the words that people said.

Name _____

Who Said That? ▶ quotation marks

Quotation marks are a type of punctuation mark used to go around the words that people say.

> **example:** "Can I borrow a pencil?" asked Hayden.

Put quotation marks around the words that people are saying in the sentences.

It's a secret, whispered Donovan.

Don't touch that! screeched Alysa.

Brenda yelled, I've got the ball!

I'm glad that's done, sighed Ms. Horn.

I understand now! exclaimed Sean.

This is the best burger ever, stated Wesley.

Yes, I can help you with that, replied Ernesto.

What is your name? asked Georgia.

You have to push this button, explained Colton.

This is fun, said Holly.

 Review Work

In the sentences, underline the verbs that are used in place of the verb *said*.

 Draft Book

Choose five verbs from above that are used in place of the verb *said*. Write a sentence with each verb. Put quotation marks around the words people say.

▶ Dear Friend ━━━━▶ friendly letters

A friendly letter has five parts: date, greeting, body, closing, and signature. A comma is needed after the greeting and closing.

August 5, 2002	← date
Dear Grandma,	← greeting
Thank you for the game! It is the one I wanted. I hope we can play it together when you come over on Sunday.	← body
Love,	← closing
Annabelle	← signature

Fill in the missing parts of the friendly letter. Label each part.

_____ , 2003   ← _____

Dear _____ ,   ← _____

   You are invited to a picnic! Let me know if you can come. I hope to see you there.   ← body
     Sincerely,   ← closing

_____   ←

🔍 **Review Work**

Underline the pronouns in the friendly letters with red.

✏️ **Draft Book**

Write a letter to a friend. Include the five parts of a friendly letter. Remember to use punctuation marks where they are needed.

Name _____

A friendly letter has five parts: date, greeting, body, closing, and signature. A comma is needed after the greeting and closing.

Tuesday, May 8, 2001	←— date
Dear Libby,	←— greeting
You are my best friend. I am glad that you like scary movies and good books.	←— body
Your friend,	←— closing
Sammy	←— signature

Add the missing punctuation marks. Label each letter part.

Monday March 24 2003	←— _____
Dear Aunt Sue	←— _____
I really liked visiting you on your farm How is your duck doing I miss him Is he staying out of trouble I hope so Say "Hi" to all of the animals for me	←— _____
Sincerely	←— _____
Mimi	←— signature

🔍 **Review Work**

Underline the nouns in the friendly letters with yellow.

✏️ **Draft Book**

Write a letter to a family member. Include the five parts of a friendly letter. Remember to use punctuation marks where they are needed.

Not Correct

The sentences below have many mistakes in them. Here are some of the mistakes you will find:

noun and verb agreement   ending punctuation
verb tenses   commas
capitalization   quotation marks

Rewrite the sentences correctly.

nathan billy theo and i is at the park

_____

mr. merman shout, someone takes my tomatoes

_____

gavin lay dig and build in the beach sand

_____

is your family drive to chicago with us

_____

i is born on tuesday august 20 1991, saying adrienne

_____

the shiny juicy yellow pears is for raul and me

_____

Name _____

▶ Many Mistakes

The friendly letter below has many mistakes in it. Here are some of the mistakes you will find:

capitalization	commas
ending punctuation	homophones
articles	pronouns

Rewrite the friendly letter correctly in your Draft Book.

---

saturday july 27 2002

dear mom

    this is your sun righting you a letter two ask a question   please

think about it before you say know   rhonda and i think us need an

dog   we promise to keep hour rooms clean   eye will walk the dog

and rhonda will feed it   it can take turns sleeping with rhonda and

me   i will save money too buy them an leash   rhonda will save his

money to buy a orange bowl   we will make sure it is not two noisy

the neighbors don't like dogs, so we will keep it out of they're yard

lots of hour friends have dogs   there parents think an dog teaches

them responsibility   will you and Dad think about it   please let

rhonda and me no by friday   if you want more time to think about

it, we can wait longer for a answer

love
ramone

Name _____

▶ Student Editing Checklist

- ☐ Each sentence tells a complete thought.
- ☐ The first word in each sentence begins with an uppercase letter.
- ☐ The pronoun I is always capitalized.
- ☐ Each word that names a day, month, or holiday starts with an uppercase letter.
- ☐ Each proper noun starts with an uppercase letter.
- ☐ Each title starts with an uppercase letter.
- ☐ Each declarative or imperative sentence ends with a period.
- ☐ Each interrogative sentence ends with a question mark.
- ☐ Each exclamatory sentence ends with an exclamation mark.
- ☐ Commas are used to separate dates.
- ☐ Commas are used in the greeting and closing in a letter.
- ☐ Commas are used in a list or series of three or more words.
- ☐ A comma is used between a city and state.
- ☐ Quotation marks go around the words that people say.
- ☐ A plural noun usually ends in *s* or *es*.
- ☐ A possessive noun usually ends in '*s*.
- ☐ Subject pronouns come before verbs.
- ☐ Object pronouns come after verbs.
- ☐ All verb tenses correctly describe when something is happening.
- ☐ Singular verbs follow singular nouns.
- ☐ Plural verbs follow plural nouns.
- ☐ Words are spelled correctly for their meanings.
- ☐ Articles are used before nouns or adjective/noun combinations.
- ☐ Apostrophes take the place of dropped letters in contractions.

Answer Key

Page 6: Answers will vary.

Page 7

Name _____

▶ **Places**   nouns

Nouns are words that name people. Nouns also name places.
 examples: garage, jungle
 examples: Grand Canyon, Australia
Circle the nouns that name places.

Jan   bear   cat   (Hawaii)

scissors   dime   (school)   truck

(France)   plate   (store)   (United States)

(home)   (classroom)   music   bird

Write the nouns that name places.

The pool is in the backyard. _____ backyard

The cat ran to the barn. _____ barn

George drove to Toronto. _____ Toronto

Stevie's class went to the zoo. _____ zoo

Max lives on Pine Street. _____ Pine Street

🔍 **Review Work**
 Find the nouns in the sentences that name people. Underline them with yellow.

✏️ **Draft Book**
 Write three sentences using nouns that name places. Underline these nouns with yellow. Draw a triangle above each of these nouns.

8 CD-4337 Grammar Rules! Grades 1–2 7   © Carson-Dellosa

RW: Underline George, Stevie, and Max with yellow. DB: Answers will vary.

Page 8

Name _____

▶ **Things**   nouns

Nouns are words that name people and places. Nouns also name things.
 examples: bird, buttons
 examples: Yankee Stadium, Statue of Liberty
The nouns below name things. Draw a picture of each one.

[ ] book   pencil

[ ] dog   shoe

Use the nouns to finish the sentences.

Meg can write with a _____ pencil

Ian likes to read his _____ book

Caleb's _____ dog _____ barked at the man.

Natalia put the _____ shoe _____ on her foot.

🔍 **Review Work**
 Find the nouns in the sentences that name people. Underline them with yellow.

✏️ **Draft Book**
 Write three sentences using nouns that name people, places, or things. Underline these nouns with yellow.

8 CD-4337 Grammar Rules! Grades 1–2   © Carson-Dellosa

Illustrate a book, pencil, dog, and shoe.
RW: Underline Meg, Ian, Caleb, and Natalia with yellow.
DB: Answers will vary.

Page 9

Name _____

▶ **ABC Order**   nouns

Nouns are words that name people, places, or things.
Look at the word pairs. Circle the noun in each pair.

(home)/ hurry   (boy)/ begin   do /(door)

(library)/ lay   (egg)/ eat   in /(ice)

(Grandma)/ great   (ant)/ eat   for /(farm)

keep /(king)   could /(cave)   join /(Jack)

Write one of the first 12 letters of the alphabet in order in each box. Write each noun from the word pairs next to the letter it starts with. Now, the nouns are in ABC order.

a	ant	g	Grandma
b	boy	h	home
c	cave	i	ice
d	door	j	Jack
e	egg	k	king
f	farm	l	library

🔍 **Review Work**
 Find the circled nouns that name people in the word pairs. Underline them with yellow.

✏️ **Draft Book**
 Write six nouns. Your nouns should name people, places, and things. Rewrite the nouns in ABC order.

CD-4337 Grammar Rules! Grades 1–2 9   © Carson-Dellosa

RW: Underline door, egg, ice, and ant with yellow. DB: Answers will vary.

Page 10

Name _____

▶ **Finish the Alphabet**   nouns

Nouns are words that name people, places, or things.
Look at the words. Circle each noun.

old   are   (quilt)   running   say   (singer)   put   (Wisconsin)

the   (zoo)   (X ray)   (teacher)   hot   (upstairs)   (rice)   (neighbor)

(yak)   ask   (mother)   (Patricia)   tell   (outside)   born   (Vermont)

Start with M and write the last 14 letters of the alphabet. Write one letter in each box. Write each noun from above next to the letter it starts with. Now, the nouns are in ABC order.

m	mother	t	teacher
n	neighbor	u	upstairs
o	outside	v	Vermont
p	Patricia	w	Wisconsin
q	quilt	x	X ray
r	rice	y	yak
s	singer	z	zoo

🔍 **Review Work**
 Find the circled nouns that name places. Draw a triangle above each of these nouns.

✏️ **Draft Book**
 Find a page of your writing. Underline the nouns in yellow. Write the nouns in ABC order.

10 CD-4337 Grammar Rules! Grades 1–2   © Carson-Dellosa

RW: Draw a triangle above Wisconsin, zoo, upstairs, outside, and Vermont.
DB: Answers will vary.

Page 11

Name _____

▶ **Categories**   nouns

Nouns are words that name people, places, or things.
Write each noun in the correct category.

ear   sister   gum
doll   baby   car
Dad   store   playground
Earth   foot   child
doctor   forest   classroom

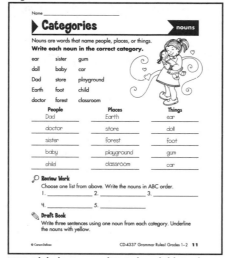

People	**Places**	**Things**
Dad	Earth	ear
doctor	store	doll
sister	forest	foot
baby	playground	gum
child	classroom	car

🔍 **Review Work**
 Choose one list from above. Write the nouns in ABC order.
 1. _____ 2. _____ 3. _____
 4. _____ 5. _____

✏️ **Draft Book**
 Write three sentences using one noun from each category. Underline the nouns with yellow.

CD-4337 Grammar Rules! Grades 1–2 11   © Carson-Dellosa

RW: Alphabetize one list. Baby, child, Dad, doctor, sister. Classroom, Earth, forest, playground, store. Car, doll, ear, foot, gum.
DB: Answers will vary.

Page 12

Name _____

▶ **Find the Nouns**   nouns

Nouns are words that name people, places, or things.
Underline the nouns.

Kira has a yellow sun on her shirt.

Chase went to the store to buy apples.

Her brother watered the plants on the deck.

Sabena placed the cupcakes on the counter.

The bike on the sidewalk belongs to my friend.

🔍 **Review Work**
 Choose two nouns from the sentences that name things. Draw a picture of each one. Write their names.

[ ]   [ ]

✏️ **Draft Book**
 Make a list of the places you go during the week. Start with your home. These words are all nouns!

12 CD-4337 Grammar Rules! Grades 1–2   © Carson-Dellosa

RW: Illustrate two "thing" nouns.
DB: Answers will vary.

Page 13

Name _____

▶ **Who Did That?**   nouns

Nouns are words that name people, places, or things.
Draw an X on each word that is not a noun.

student   dripping   carpenter   doctor   more   over   librarian

walked   firefighter   teacher   write   clerk   chef   ✗

Use some of the nouns to finish the sentences.

The _____ doctor _____ gave Tonya a checkup.

The _____ carpenter _____ built a new house for Audrey.

The _____ teacher _____ helps Ross measure with a ruler.

The _____ chef _____ cooked the food in the restaurant.

The _____ librarian _____ helps Rita check out books.

The _____ firefighter _____ put out the fire in the building.

🔍 **Review Work**
 Find the other nouns in the sentences. Underline them with yellow.

✏️ **Draft Book**
 Two of the nouns were not used in the sentences. Write a sentence with each one.

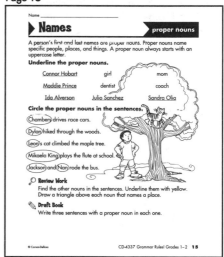

CD-4337 Grammar Rules! Grades 1–2 13   © Carson-Dellosa

RW: Underline Tonya, checkup, house, Audrey, Ross, ruler, food, restaurant, Rita, books, fire, and building with yellow. DB: Answers will vary.
Page 14: Draw lines from ruler, chalk, crayon, book, scissors, pencil, and paper to the desk.
RW: Underline birds, cage, lizard, elephant, lion, path, and tiger. DB: Answers will vary.

Page 15

Name _____

▶ **Names**   proper nouns

A person's first and last names are proper nouns. Proper nouns name specific people, places, and things. A proper noun always starts with an uppercase letter.
Underline the proper nouns.

Connor Hobart   girl   mom

Maddie Prince   dentist   coach

Ida Alverson   Julio Sanchez   Sandra Olia

Circle the proper nouns in the sentences.

(Chambers) drives race cars.

(Dylan) hiked through the woods.

(Leon)'s cat climbed the maple tree.

(Mikaela King) plays the flute at school.

(Jackson) and (Nan) rode the bus.

🔍 **Review Work**
 Find the other nouns in the sentences. Underline them with yellow. Draw a triangle above each noun that names a place.

✏️ **Draft Book**
 Write three sentences with a proper noun in each one.

© Carson-Dellosa   CD-4337 Grammar Rules! Grades 1–2 15

RW: Underline cars, woods, cat, tree, flute, school, and bus with yellow. Draw a triangle above woods and school. DB: Answers will vary.

Page 16

Name _____

▶ **Put Those Titles On**   proper nouns

A person's first and last names are proper nouns. Proper nouns also include titles, like Mr., Mrs., Miss, Ms., and Dr. A proper noun always starts with an uppercase letter.
Rewrite the sentences correctly.

Is ms. smith your teacher?
 Is Ms. Smith your teacher?

cameron kendell, sr. is my father.
 Cameron Kendell, Sr. is my father.

Did deidre visit dr. molnar?
 Did Deidre visit Dr. Molnar?

leo marion, jr. is leo's full name.
 Leo Marion, Jr. is Leo's full name.

mr. and mrs. otten are her parents.
 Mr. and Mrs. Otten are her parents.

🔍 **Review Work**
 Underline all of the nouns in the sentences with yellow.

✏️ **Draft Book**
 Write four sentences. Include a proper noun and a title in each one.

16 CD-4337 Grammar Rules! Grades 1–2   © Carson-Dellosa

Page 16 (cont.)
RW: Underline Ms. Smith; teacher; Cameron Kendell, Sr.; father; Deidre; Dr. Molnar; Leo Marion, Jr.; Leo; name; Mr. and Mrs. Otten; and parents with yellow.
DB: Answers will vary.

Page 17

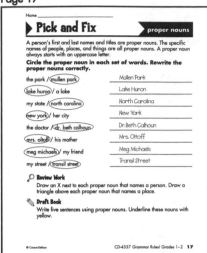

Pick and Fix — proper nouns

A person's first and last names and titles are proper nouns. The specific names of people, places, and things are all proper nouns. A proper noun always starts with an uppercase letter.

Circle the proper noun in each set of words. Rewrite the proper nouns correctly.

the park /(mullen park)	Mullen Park
(lake huron) / a lake	Lake Huron
my state /(north carolina)	North Carolina
(new york) / her city	New York
the doctor /(dr. beth calhoun)	Dr Beth Calhoun
(mrs. oltoff) / his mother	Mrs. Oltoff
(meg michaels) / my friend	Meg Michaels
my street /(transil street)	Transil Street

Review Work
Draw an X next to each proper noun that names a person. Draw a triangle above each proper noun that names a place.

Draft Book
Write five sentences using proper nouns. Underline these nouns with yellow.

© Carson-Dellosa   CD-4337 Grammar Rules! Grades 1–2   17

RW: Draw an X next to Dr. Beth Calhoun, Mrs. Oltoff, and Meg Michaels. Draw a triangle above Mullen Park, Lake Huron, North Carolina, New York, and Transil Street.
DB: Answers will vary.

Page 18

Addresses — proper nouns

Proper nouns name specific people, places, and things. A proper noun always starts with an uppercase letter. When proper nouns name a city and state, a comma goes between them.
example: Orlando, Florida

Write the names and addresses correctly. Capitalize the proper nouns. Put a comma between each city name and state name.

mr. cody stoneson
461 oak avenue
littletown ohio 12345

Mr. Cody Stoneson
461 Oak Avenue
Littletown, Ohio 12345

dr. coral sargasso
876 waterway boulevard
kelp maine 13579

Dr Coral Sargasso
876 Waterway Boulevard
Kelp, Maine 13579

Review Work
Draw an X next to each proper noun that names a person.

Draft Book
Write your name and address. Capitalize all of the proper nouns. Put a comma between the names of your city and state.

18   CD-4337 Grammar Rules! Grades 1–2   © Carson-Dellosa

RW: Draw an X next to Mr. Cody Stoneson and Dr. Coral Sargasso.
DB: Answers will vary.

Page 19

Special Times — proper nouns

Days, months, and holidays are proper nouns. A proper noun always starts with an uppercase letter.
Look at the words. Cross out the first letter of each proper noun and write an uppercase letter above it.

S   P   D   M
st. patrick's day   monday   T
                          thanksgiving
presents   S   J
          sunday   july
N   Y   D   A
new year's day   august   hearts
H   F   J
hanukkah   turkey   january
S   F   C
saturday   february   christmas
O   C   N
october   calendar   november
T   S   D
tuesday   leprechaun   december
W   V   D   T
wednesday   valentine's day   thursday

Review Work
Write a sentence about your favorite month or holiday.

Draft Book
Write two sentences using nouns that name days, months, and holidays. Underline these nouns with yellow.

© Carson-Dellosa   CD-4337 Grammar Rules! Grades 1–2   19

RW: Answers will vary.   DB: Answers will vary.
Page 20
Draw lines to match months and days with their abbreviations. RW: 1. Sunday 2. Monday 3. Tuesday 4. Wednesday 5. Thursday 6. Friday 7. Saturday.

Page 21

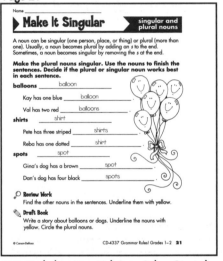

Make It Singular — singular and plural nouns

A noun can be singular (one person, place, or thing) or plural (more than one). Usually, a noun becomes plural by adding an s to the end. Sometimes, a noun becomes singular by removing the s at the end.

Make the plural nouns singular. Use the nouns to finish the sentences. Decide if the plural or singular noun works best in each sentence.

balloons _____ balloon

Kay has one blue _____ balloon

Val has two red _____ balloons

shirts _____ shirt

Pete has three striped _____ shirts

Reba has one dotted _____ shirt

spots _____ spot

Gina's dog has a brown _____ spot

Dan's dog has four black _____ spots

Review Work
Find the other nouns in the sentences. Underline them with yellow.

Draft Book
Write a story about balloons or dogs. Underline the nouns with yellow. Circle the plural nouns.

© Carson-Dellosa   CD-4337 Grammar Rules! Grades 1–2   21

RW: Underline Kay, Val, Pete, Reba, Gina, dog, Dan, and dog with yellow. DB: Answers will vary.
Page 22

Lots of Shapes — plural nouns

A noun can be singular (one person, place, or thing) or plural (more than one). Usually, a noun becomes plural by adding an s to the end.
Make the nouns plural. Add to each picture to show more than one shape.

circle _____ square _____
circles   squares

More shapes should have been added to each picture.

triangle _____ oval _____
triangles   ovals

Review Work
Write the plural nouns in ABC order.
1. _____ circles   2. _____ ovals
3. _____ squares   4. _____ triangles

Draft Book
Make these nouns plural: rectangle, star, diamond, octagon.
rectangles, stars, diamonds, octagons

22   CD-4337 Grammar Rules! Grades 1–2   © Carson-Dellosa

Page 23

Critters — plural nouns

A noun can be singular (one person, place, or thing) or plural (more than one). Usually, a noun becomes plural by adding an s to the end.
Make the nouns plural.

bee _____ bees
frog _____ frogs
turtle _____ turtles
dog _____ dogs
snail _____ snails

Use the plural nouns to finish the sentences.

Two _____ turtles _____ were sitting on a log.
Three _____ bees _____ visited the flower.
Four _____ frogs _____ were on lily pads.
Five _____ snails _____ were on the ground.
Six _____ dogs _____ were barking at cats.

Review Work
Find the other nouns in the sentences. Underline them with yellow.

Draft Book
Write a story about frogs jumping over a log. Underline the nouns with yellow.

© Carson-Dellosa   CD-4337 Grammar Rules! Grades 1–2   23

RW: Underline log, flower, lily pads, ground, and cats with yellow.
DB: Answers will vary.

Page 24

Party Time — plural nouns

A noun can be singular (one person, place, or thing) or plural (more than one). Sometimes, a noun becomes plural by adding es to the end.
example: beach → beaches   example: brush → brushes
example: dress → dresses   example: ox → axes
Make the nouns plural by adding es to the end.

box _____ boxes   wish _____ wishes
dish _____ dishes   glass _____ glasses

Use the plural nouns to finish the sentences.

A magic frog gave Dante three _____ wishes _____.
Dante wished for ten _____ dishes _____ of ice cream.
He also wished for ten _____ glasses _____ of milk.
His last wish was for ten _____ boxes _____ of cookies.
Now, Dante will have a party!

Review Work
Find the other nouns in the sentences. Underline them with yellow.

Draft Book
Write a story about a party you have been to. Underline the nouns with yellow. Circle the plural nouns.

24   CD-4337 Grammar Rules! Grades 1–2   © Carson-Dellosa

RW: Underline frog, Dante, ice cream, milk, wish, cookies, and party with yellow.
DB: Answers will vary

Page 25

Nature Walk — plural nouns

A noun can be singular (one person, place, or thing) or plural (more than one). Sometimes, a noun becomes plural by adding es to the end.
example: beach → beaches   example: brush → brushes
example: dress → dresses   example: ox → axes
Make the nouns plural by adding s or es to the end.

bird _____ birds   bug _____ bugs
fox _____ foxes   peach _____ peaches
horse _____ horses   tree _____ trees
flower _____ flowers   branch _____ branches
bush _____ bushes   plant _____ plants

Review Work
Choose a noun from the list. Write the singular form on the first line and the plural form on the second line. Draw a picture to show each word.

Draft Book
Write a story about a time you went on a walk outside. Underline the nouns with yellow. Circle the plural nouns.

© Carson-Dellosa   CD-4337 Grammar Rules! Grades 1–2   25

RW: Answers will vary.
DB: Answers will vary.

Page 26

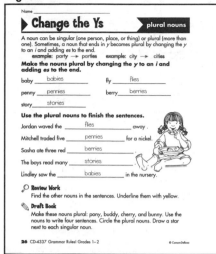

Change the Ys — plural nouns

A noun can be singular (one person, place, or thing) or plural (more than one). Sometimes, a noun that ends in *y* becomes plural by changing the *y* to an *i* and adding *es* to the end.
example: party → parties   example: city → cities
Make the nouns plural by changing the *y* to an *i* and adding *es* to the end.

baby ___babies___   fly ___flies___
penny ___pennies___   berry ___berries___
story ___stories___

Use the plural nouns to finish the sentences.
Jordan waved the ___flies___ away.
Mitchell traded five ___pennies___ for a nickel.
Sasha ate three red ___berries___
The boys read many ___stories___
Lindley saw the ___babies___ in the nursery.

🔍 **Review Work**
Find the other nouns in the sentences. Underline them with yellow.

✏️ **Draft Book**
Make these nouns plural: pony, buddy, cherry, and bunny. Use the nouns to write four sentences. Circle the plural nouns. Draw a star next to each singular noun.

26 CD-4337 Grammar Rules! Grades 1–2

RW: Underline Jordan, Mitchell, nickel, Sasha, boys, Lindley, and nursery.
DB: Ponies, buddies, cherries, bunnies. Answers will vary.

Page 27

Tricky Nouns — other plural nouns

A noun can be singular (one person, place, or thing) or plural (more than one). Some nouns become plural by making changes in the middles or at the ends.
Draw lines to match the singular and plural nouns.

goose — children
mouse — people
tooth — feet
child — leaves
foot — women
person — mice
man — geese
woman — halves
leaf — men
half — teeth

Circle the tricky nouns in the sentences.
We cut the candy bars into (halves).
(Men), (women), and (children) are all (people).
A (goose) has two (feet). Four (geese) have eight (feet).
(Mice) have sharp (teeth).
Many (leaves) are on that tree.

🔍 **Review Work**
Find the other nouns in the sentences. Underline them with yellow.

✏️ **Draft Book**
Write a story using some of the nouns above. Circle the plural nouns. Draw a star next to each singular noun.

© Carson-Dellosa   CD-4337 Grammar Rules! Grades 1–2 **27**

Draw lines to match goose/geese, mouse/mice, tooth/teeth, child/children, foot/feet, person/people, man/men, woman/women, leaf/leaves, and half/halves.
RW: Underline candy bars and tree.
DB: Answers will vary.

Page 28

How Many in All? — plural noun review

Use the plural form of the nouns to fill in the sentences.

example: penny   cup
There are six ___pennies___ in the two ___cups___.

mouse   room
There are two ___mice___ in the three ___rooms___

child   bench
There are four ___children___ on the two ___benches___

blueberry   dish
There are five ___blueberries___ in the two ___dishes___

nut   box
There are six ___nuts___ in the four ___boxes___

🔍 **Review Work**
Make these nouns plural: church, brush, fairy.
churches, brushes, fairies

✏️ **Draft Book**
Write a story using some of the nouns above. Circle the plural nouns. Draw a star next to each singular noun.

28 CD-4337 Grammar Rules! Grades 1–2   © Carson-Dellosa

DB: Answers will vary.

Page 29

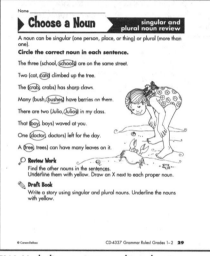

Choose a Noun — singular and plural noun review

A noun can be singular (one person, place, or thing) or plural (more than one).
Circle the correct noun in each sentence.
The three (school, (schools)) are on the same street.
Two (cat, (cats)) climbed up the tree.
The ((crab), crabs) has sharp claws.
Many (bush, (bushes)) have berries on them.
There are two ((Julio), Julios) in my class.
That ((boy), boys) waved at you.
One ((doctor), doctors) left for the day.
A ((tree), trees) can have many leaves on it.

🔍 **Review Work**
Find the other nouns in the sentences. Underline them with yellow. Draw an X next to each proper noun.

✏️ **Draft Book**
Write a story using singular and plural nouns. Underline the nouns with yellow.

© Carson-Dellosa   CD-4337 Grammar Rules! Grades 1–2 **29**

RW: Underline street, tree, claws, berries, class, day, leaves with yellow. Draw an X next to Julio.
DB: Answers will vary.

Page 30

Mine, All Mine — possessive nouns

A possessive noun shows that something belongs to someone. Usually, a noun becomes possessive by adding *'s* to the end.
Finish each sentence with a possessive noun. The first one has been done for you.
The game belongs to my brother. It is my ___brother's___ game.
The pencils belong to Li. Those are ___Li's___ pencils.
That necklace belongs to Mom. It is ___Mom's___ necklace.
The pennies belong to Juan. Those are ___Juan's___ pennies.
That horse belongs to Rosa. It is ___Rosa's___ horse.
The hamster belongs to Tito. It is ___Tito's___ hamster.

🔍 **Review Work**
Write two singular and two plural nouns from the sentences above.
singular nouns   plural nouns
_____   _____
_____   _____

✏️ **Draft Book**
Choose three friends. Use possessive nouns to write sentences about things that belong to them. Write one sentence about each friend.

30 CD-4337 Grammar Rules! Grades 1–2   © Carson-Dellosa

RW: Answers will vary. DB: Answers will vary.

Page 31

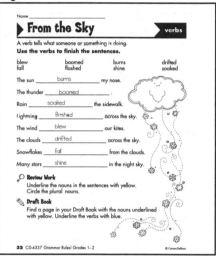

Family Fun — verbs

A verb tells what someone or something is doing.
example: The boy *swings* the golf club.
example: The car *races* around the racetrack.
Underline the verbs in blue.
My sister Emily (slides) down the slide.
My dad (pushes) Paige on the merry-go-round.
My brother Hal (climbs) the big tree.
My grandmother (sits) on the bench.
My grandfather (hits) the ball with a racket.
My mom (catches) Emily at the bottom.
I (swing) across the monkey bars.

🔍 **Review Work**
Underline the nouns in the sentences with yellow.

✏️ **Draft Book**
Find a page in your Draft Book with the nouns underlined with yellow. Underline the verbs with blue.

© Carson-Dellosa   CD-4337 Grammar Rules! Grades 1–2 **31**

RW: Underline sister, Emily, slide, mom, Emily, bottom, brother, Hal, tree, grandmother, bench, grandfather, ball, racket, dad, Paige, merry-go-round, and monkey bars with yellow.
DB: Answers will vary.

Page 32

From the Sky — verbs

A verb tells what someone or something is doing.
Use the verbs to finish the sentences.
blew   boomed   burns   drifted
fall   flashed   shine   soaked

The sun ___burns___ my nose.
The thunder ___boomed___
Rain ___soaked___ the sidewalk.
Lightning ___flashed___ across the sky.
The wind ___blew___ our kites.
The clouds ___drifted___ across the sky.
Snowflakes ___fall___ from the clouds.
Many stars ___shine___ in the night sky.

🔍 **Review Work**
Underline the nouns in the sentences with yellow. Circle the plural nouns.

✏️ **Draft Book**
Find a page in your Draft Book with the nouns underlined with yellow. Underline the verbs with blue.

32 CD-4337 Grammar Rules! Grades 1–2   © Carson-Dellosa

RW: Underline sun, nose, thunder, rain, sidewalk, lightning, sky, wind, kites, clouds, sky, snowflakes, clouds, stars, and sky with yellow. Circle kites, clouds, snowflakes, clouds, and stars.
DB: Answers will vary.

Page 33
Draw lines to match pictures.
RW: Underline clown, balloons, children, seals, balls, noses, man, treats, and cotton candy with yellow. Draw a star above clown, man, and cotton candy.
DB: Answers will vary.

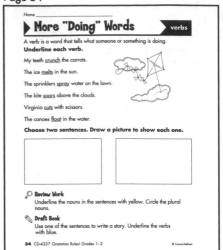

More "Doing" Words — verbs

A verb is a word that tells what someone or something is doing.

Underline each verb.

My teeth crunch the carrots.

The ice melts in the sun.

The sprinklers spray water on the lawn.

The kite soars above the clouds.

Virginia cuts with scissors.

The canoes float in the water.

Choose two sentences. Draw a picture to show each one.

Review Work
Underline the nouns in the sentences with yellow. Circle the plural nouns.

Draft Book
Use one of the sentences to write a story. Underline the verbs with blue.

34 CD-4337 Grammar Rules! Grades 1–2 © Carson-Dellosa

Illustrate two sentences.
RW: Underline teeth, carrots, ice, sun, sprinklers, water, lawn, kite, clouds, Virginia, scissors, canoes, and water with yellow. Circle teeth, carrots, sprinklers, clouds, scissors, and canoes. DB: Answers will vary.

Page 35

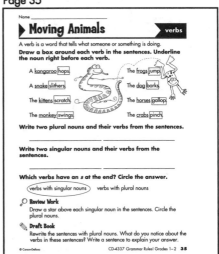

Moving Animals — verbs

A verb is a word that tells what someone or something is doing.

Draw a box around each verb in the sentences. Underline the noun right before each verb.

A kangaroo hops. The frogs jump.

A snake slithers. The dog barks.

The kittens scratch. The horses gallop.

The monkey swings. The crabs pinch.

Write two plural nouns and their verbs from the sentences.

Write two singular nouns and their verbs from the sentences.

Which verbs have an s at the end? Circle the answer.
verbs with singular nouns / verbs with plural nouns

Review Work
Draw a star above each singular noun in the sentences. Circle the plural nouns.

Draft Book
Rewrite the sentences with plural nouns. What do you notice about the verbs in these sentences? Write a sentence to explain your answer.

© Carson-Dellosa CD-4337 Grammar Rules! Grades 1–2 35

Plural nouns and verbs will vary. Singular nouns and verbs will vary.
RW: Draw a star above kangaroo, snake, monkey, and dog. Circle kittens, frogs, horses, and crabs.
DB: Answers will vary.

Page 36

Sweet Stuff — noun and verb agreement

A singular noun uses a verb that has an s at the end. A plural noun uses a verb that does not have an s at the end.
example: The firefighter climbs the ladder. (singular noun and verb)
example: The firefighters climb the ladder. (plural noun and verb)
Circle the correct verb in each sentence.

Serena (plant, plants) the seeds.

The seeds (grow, grows) into flowers.

The bees (visit, visits) the flowers.

The bees (fly, flies) back to the hive.

The bees (make, makes) honey.

The beekeeper (collect, collects) the honey.

The grocery store (sell, sells) the honey.

Serena's father (buy, buys) honey.

The children (eat, eats) the honey on bread.

Review Work
Underline the nouns in the sentences with yellow.

Draft Book
Use one of the sentences to write a story. Underline the verbs with blue. Underline the nouns with yellow.

36 CD-4337 Grammar Rules! Grades 1–2 © Carson-Dellosa

RW: Underline Serena, seeds, seeds, flowers, bees, flowers, bees, hive, bees, honey, beekeeper, honey, grocery store, honey, Serena, father, honey, children, honey, and bread with yellow. DB: Answers will vary.

Page 37

Sea Life — noun and verb agreement

A singular noun uses a verb that has an s at the end. A plural noun uses a verb that does not have an s at the end.
example: The girl runs in the race. (singular noun and verb)
example: The girls run in the race. (plural noun and verb)
Use the verbs to finish the sentences. Add an s to the ends of the words if needed.

crawl hide jump snap swim

The three dolphins **jump** out of the water.

The eel **hides** behind the rocks.

A fish **swims** through the water.

The clams **snap** their shells shut.

The crab **crawls** across the ocean floor.

Review Work
Underline the nouns in the sentences with yellow. Draw a star above each singular noun.

Draft Book
Write a story about a sea creature. Underline the verbs with blue. Underline the nouns with yellow.

CD-4337 Grammar Rules! Grades 1–2 37

RW: Underline dolphins, water, eel, rocks, fish, water, clams, shells, crab, and floor with yellow. Draw a star above water, eel, fish, water, crab, and floor. DB: Answers will vary.

Page 38

Sounds — noun and verb agreement

A singular noun uses a verb that has an s at the end. A plural noun uses a verb that does not have an s at the end.
example: The cat meows at my brother. (singular noun and verb)
example: The cats meow at my brother. (plural noun and verb)
Choose the correct noun and verb to finish each sentence. Write the words on the lines.

That **girl** **yells** loudly.
girl / girls yell / yells

The three **birds** **sing** a pretty song.
bird / birds sings / sing

Those **dogs** **bark** at the children.
dog / dogs barks / bark

A **glass** **crashes** when it falls.
glass / glasses crash / crashes

That **boy** **whistles** well.
boy / boys whistle / whistles

Review Work
Underline the nouns in the sentences with yellow. Circle the plural nouns.

Draft Book
Write a story about noises. Underline the verbs with blue. Underline the nouns with yellow. Make sure your nouns and verbs agree.

38 CD-4337 Grammar Rules! Grades 1–2 © Carson-Dellosa

Page 38 (cont.)
RW: Underline girl, birds, song, dogs, children, glass, and boy with yellow. Circle birds, dogs, and children. DB: Answers will vary.

Page 39

Let's Exercise — past and present tense

Verbs use tenses to tell when something is happening. When the action happens now, it is present tense. When the action happened before, it is past tense. One way to make a verb past tense is to add ed to the end.
Underline the present tense verb in the first sentence. Add ed to make the verb past tense in the second sentence.

The boys play baseball.

Last week, the boys **played** baseball.

The girls walk to the park.

Yesterday, the girls **walked** to the park.

The players kick the soccer ball.

In the last game, the players **kicked** the soccer ball.

The runners race to the finish line.

An hour ago, the runners **raced** to the finish line.

Review Work
Circle the plural nouns in the sentences.

Draft Book
Find a story you wrote. Draw a box around each verb with an ed ending.

CD-4337 Grammar Rules! Grades 1–2 39

RW: Circle boys, girls, players, and runners. DB: Answers will vary.

Page 40

Cooking — past and present tense

Verbs use tenses to tell when something is happening. When the action happens now, it is present tense. When the action happened before, it is past tense. One way to make a verb past tense is to add ed to the end. If the noun is singular, take off the s or es at the end of the verb before adding ed.
Underline the present tense verb in the first sentence. Add ed to make the verb past tense in the second sentence.

Grandma bakes great cookies.

Last week, Grandma **baked** brownies.

Grandpa grills hamburgers.

Yesterday, Grandpa **grilled** hot dogs.

Dad rolls the dough for cinnamon rolls.

Last night, Dad **rolled** the dough for cookies.

Mom mixes the batter for pancakes.

Last Tuesday, Mom **mixed** the fruit salad.

Review Work
Draw a star above each singular noun in the sentences.

Draft Book
Find a story you wrote. Draw a box around each verb with an ed ending.

40 CD-4337 Grammar Rules! Grades 1–2 © Carson-Dellosa

RW: Draw a star above Grandma, Grandpa, Dad, dough, Mom, batter, and fruit salad. DB: Answers will vary.

Page 41

Verb Tenses — past and present tense

Verbs use tenses to tell when something is happening. When the action happens now, it is present tense. When the action happened before, it is past tense.
Circle the correct verb in each sentence.

Orlando (brushes, brush, brushed) his dog yesterday.

In the past, the glue (dried, dries, dry) quickly.

Mia (save, saved, saves) pennies for almost a year.

Last week, we (pick, picks, picked) blueberries.

He (flattens, flattened, flatten) the clay to make the project.

Trey (collected, collects, collect) 100 toy cars last year.

Anna and Courtney (tie, ties, tied) their shoes before they played.

Last summer, the sprinklers (waters, watered, water) the grass.

Review Work
Underline the nouns in the sentences with yellow.

Draft Book
Choose one of the sentences and write a story. Use some verbs with ed endings. Draw a box around each verb with an ed ending. Underline any other verbs with blue.

CD-4337 Grammar Rules! Grades 1–2 41

Page 41 (cont).
RW: Underline Orlando, dog, glue, Mia, pennies, year, week, blueberries, clay, project, Trey, cars, year, Anna, Courtney, shoes, summer, sprinklers, and grass.
DB: Answers will vary.

Page 42

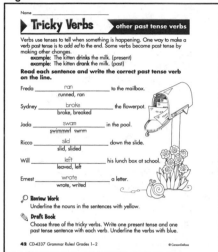

> ► **Tricky Verbs** other past tense verbs
>
> Name _____
>
> Verbs use tenses to tell when something is happening. One way to make a verb past tense is to add *ed* to the end. Some verbs become past tense by making other changes.
> **example:** The kitten drinks the milk. (present)
> **example:** The kitten drank the milk. (past)
> **Read each sentence and write the correct past tense verb on the line.**
>
> Freda ___ran___ to the mailbox.
> runned, ran
>
> Sydney ___broke___ the flowerpot.
> broke, breaked
>
> Jada ___swam___ in the pool.
> swimmed, swim
>
> Ricco ___slid___ down the slide.
> slid, slided
>
> Will ___left___ his lunch box at school.
> leaved, left
>
> Ernest ___wrote___ a letter.
> wrote, writed
>
> 🔍 **Review Work**
> Underline the nouns in the sentences with yellow.
>
> ✎ **Draft Book**
> Choose three of the tricky verbs. Write one present tense and one past tense sentence with each verb. Underline the verbs with blue.
>
> © Carson-Dellosa   42 CD-4337 Grammar Rules! Grades 1–2

RW: Underline Freda, mailbox, Sydney, flowerpot, Ricco, slide, Jada, pool, Will, lunch box, school, Ernest, and letter with yellow.
DB: Answers will vary.

Page 43

> ► **In the Backyard** future tense
>
> Name _____
>
> Verbs use tenses to tell when something is happening. When the action will happen in the future, it is future tense. The helping verb *will* is added before the main verb to make it future tense. If the noun is singular, take off the *s* or *es* at the end of the verb before adding *will*.
> **example:** Mom eats dinner. (present)
> **example:** Mom will eat dinner. (future)
> **Underline the present tense verb in the first sentence. Add *will* to make the verb future tense in the second sentence.**
>
> Dwayne mows the lawn.
> Dwayne ___will mow___ the lawn.
>
> The crickets chirp.
> The crickets ___will chirp___.
>
> The chipmunks run into the woods.
> The chipmunks ___will run___ into the woods.
>
> Dad plants beans and carrots.
> Dad ___will plant___ beans and carrots.
>
> 🔍 **Review Work**
> Underline the nouns in the sentences with yellow.
>
> ✎ **Draft Book**
> Write four sentences using verbs in the future tense. Remember to put the helping verb *will* in front of each verb. Underline each verb with blue (including the word *will*).
>
> © Carson-Dellosa   CD-4337 Grammar Rules! Grades 1–2 43

RW: Underline Dwayne, lawn, crickets, chipmunks, woods, Dad, beans, and carrots with yellow.
DB: Answers will vary.

Page 44

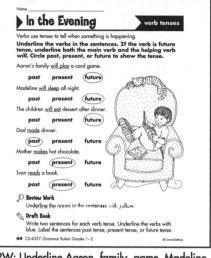

> ► **In the Evening** verb tenses
>
> Name _____
>
> Verbs use tenses to tell when something is happening.
> **Underline the verbs in the sentences. If the verb is future tense, underline both the main verb and the helping verb *will*. Circle past, present, or future to show the tense.**
>
> Aaron's family will play a card game.
> past present (future)
>
> Madeline will sleep all night.
> past present (future)
>
> The children will eat dessert after dinner.
> past present (future)
>
> Dad made dinner.
> (past) present future
>
> Mother makes hot chocolate.
> past (present) future
>
> Ivan reads a book.
> past (present) future
>
> 🔍 **Review Work**
> Underline the nouns in the sentences with yellow.
>
> ✎ **Draft Book**
> Write two sentences for each verb tense. Underline the verbs with blue. Label the sentences past tense, present tense, or future tense.
>
> 44 CD-4337 Grammar Rules! Grades 1–2   © Carson-Dellosa

RW: Underline Aaron, family, game, Madeline, night, children, dessert, dinner, Dad, dinner, Mother, hot chocolate, Ivan, and book with yellow.
DB: Answers will vary.

Page 45

> ► **Rocks and Minerals** linking verbs
>
> Name _____
>
> Linking verbs are verbs that do not show action. They express a state of being (*to be*). A linking verb connects, or links, two parts of a sentence. Some common linking verbs are am, is, are, and was.
> **example:** I am left-handed. **example:** He is an artist.
> **example:** You are a gymnast. **example:** We are best friends.
> **Underline the linking verbs in the sentences.**
>
> I am a rock collector.
>
> My collection is very big.
>
> That rock is black with little gold specks.
>
> That is a pretty rock.
>
> Rocks are fun to collect.
>
> A diamond is a mineral.
>
> Jade is a green mineral.
>
> These are rare minerals.
>
> 🔍 **Review Work**
> Underline the nouns in the sentences with yellow.
>
> ✎ **Draft Book**
> Write five sentences that use linking verbs. Underline the linking verbs with blue.
>
> © Carson-Dellosa   CD-4337 Grammar Rules! Grades 1–2 45

RW: Underline collector, collection, rock, specks, rock, rocks, diamond, mineral, Jade, mineral, and minerals with yellow.
DB: Answers will vary.

Page 46

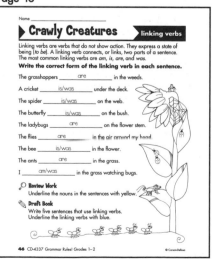

> ► **Crawly Creatures** linking verbs
>
> Name _____
>
> Linking verbs are verbs that do not show action. They express a state of being (*to be*). A linking verb connects, or links, two parts of a sentence. The most common linking verbs are am, is, are, and was.
> **Write the correct form of the linking verb in each sentence.**
>
> The grasshoppers ___are___ in the weeds.
>
> A cricket ___is/was___ under the deck.
>
> The spider ___is/was___ on the web.
>
> The butterfly ___is/was___ on the bush.
>
> The ladybugs ___are___ on the flower stem.
>
> The flies ___are___ in the air around my head.
>
> The bee ___is/was___ in the flower.
>
> The ants ___are___ in the grass.
>
> I ___am/was___ in the grass watching bugs.
>
> 🔍 **Review Work**
> Underline the nouns in the sentences with yellow.
>
> ✎ **Draft Book**
> Write five sentences that use linking verbs. Underline the linking verbs with blue.
>
> 46 CD-4337 Grammar Rules! Grades 1–2   © Carson-Dellosa

Page 46 (cont.)
RW: Underline grasshoppers, weeds, cricket, deck, spider, web, butterfly, bush, ladybugs, stem, flies, air, head, bee, flower, ants, grass, and bugs with yellow.
DB: Answers will vary.

Page 47

> ► **Numbers and Colors** adjectives
>
> Name _____
>
> Adjectives are words that describe nouns. Adjectives can tell number or color.
> **example:** Susan ate two pieces of candy.
> **example:** The yellow pear was in the basket.
> **Circle the number and color adjectives in the sentences.**
>
> Mariella collected (twenty) fireflies in the jar.
>
> Bev's rabbit ate (four) carrots.
>
> The (brown) horses galloped.
>
> Landon gathered (sixteen) pencils.
>
> Gabe picked the (yellow) flower.
>
> Ashley only ate the (green) grapes.
>
> Zelda has a (purple) headband.
>
> Carlos spent (nine) dimes.
>
> Many starfish have (five) legs.
>
> 🔍 **Review Work**
> Underline the nouns in the sentences with yellow. Draw an X next to each proper noun.
>
> ✎ **Draft Book**
> Write five sentences. Use color and number adjectives to describe the nouns.
>
> © Carson-Dellosa   CD-4337 Grammar Rules! Grades 1–2 47

RW: Underline Mariella, fireflies, jar, Bev, rabbit, carrots, horses, Landon, pencils, Gabe, flower, Ashley, grapes, Zelda, headband, Carlos, dimes, starfish, and legs with yellow. Draw an X next to Mariella, Bev, Landon, Gabe, Ashley, Zelda, and Carlos.
DB: Answers will vary.

Page 48

> ► **Size and Shape** adjectives
>
> Name _____
>
> Adjectives are words that describe nouns. Adjectives can tell size or shape.
> **example:** Jillian bought the square picture frame.
> **example:** The little boy climbed the rope.
> **Circle the size and shape adjectives in the sentences.**
>
> The (circular) clock is in the hallway.
>
> Vinny washed the (square) window.
>
> Carrie bought the (thin) ribbon.
>
> Look at that (small) sand castle.
>
> Yuri has an (oval) skateboard.
>
> Get the dog's (long) leash.
>
> Terrell caught a (tiny) fish!
>
> Hannah found her (round) glasses.
>
> Mae's (large) bucket is full of sand.
>
> That (large) spider escaped from its cage!
>
> 🔍 **Review Work**
> Underline the verbs in the sentences with blue.
>
> ✎ **Draft Book**
> Write five sentences. Use size and shape adjectives to describe the nouns.
>
> 48 CD-4337 Grammar Rules! Grades 1–2   © Carson-Dellosa

RW: Underline is, washed, bought, look, has, get, caught, found, is, and escaped with blue.
DB: Answers will vary.

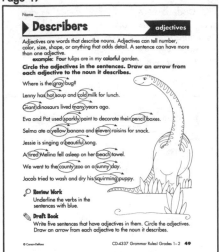

Describers — adjectives

Adjectives are words that describe nouns. Adjectives can tell number, color, size, shape, or anything that describes. A sentence can have more than one adjective.
example: Four tulips are in my colorful garden.
Circle the adjectives in the sentences. Draw an arrow from each adjective to the noun it describes.

Where is the gray bug?

Lenny has hot soup and cold milk for lunch.

Giant dinosaurs lived many years ago.

Eva and Pat used sparkly paint to decorate their pencil boxes.

Selma ate a yellow banana and eleven raisins for snack.

Jessie is singing a beautiful song.

A tired Melina fell asleep on her beach towel.

We went to the county zoo on a sunny day.

Jacob tried to wash and dry his squirming puppy.

🔍 **Review Work**
Underline the verbs in the sentences with blue.

✏️ **Draft Book**
Write five sentences that have adjectives in them. Circle the adjectives. Draw an arrow from each adjective to the noun it describes.

© Carson-Dellosa   CD-4337 Grammar Rules! Grades 1–2   **49**

RW: Underline is, has, lived, used, ate, is singing, fell, went, and tried with blue.
DB: Answers will vary.
Page 50

More Describers — adjectives

Adjectives are words that describe nouns. Adjectives can tell number, color, size, shape, or anything that adds detail.
Circle the adjectives.

heavy   walked   old   house   loose   book   shoe
twelve   sneezed   dry   star   broken   sing   whale
silly   hairy   blue   school   strong   parked   wrinkled
gold   wiggle   new   awful   friend   tired   blink

Use the adjectives to finish the sentences. Or, write your own adjectives on the lines.

Whitney held that _____ snake.

Jo broke that _____ lamp.

Charlie tried to lift the _____ lamb.

Bailey rode his _____ scooter.

🔍 **Review Work**
In the word list, underline the nouns with yellow and the verbs with blue.

✏️ **Draft Book**
Write five sentences that have adjectives in them. Circle the adjectives. Draw an arrow from each adjective to the noun it describes.

50 CD-4337 Grammar Rules! Grades 1–2   © Carson-Dellosa

Sentence adjectives will vary.
RW: Underline house, book, shoe, star, whale, school, and friend with yellow. Underline walked, sneezed, sing, parked, wiggle, and blink with blue. DB: Answers will vary.
Page 51

Mixed-Up Words — nouns, verbs, and adjectives

Sometimes a word that is a noun in one sentence can be a verb or an adjective in another sentence. How the word is used in a sentence determines what type of word it is.
example: That fly is bothering me. (noun)
example: I fly my kite. (verb)
example: Jamie caught the fly ball. (adjective)
What type of word is the underlined word in each sentence? Write noun, verb, or adjective on each line.

I comb the tangles out of my hair.   verb

Riley has a red comb.   noun

Cassidy likes cherry pie.   adjective

I want to eat that cherry.   noun

The fruit bat hangs upside down to sleep.   noun

Juan and Jo bat the ball over the fence.   verb

Turn on the light.   noun

Gerry carried the light bag.   adjective

🔍 **Review Work**
Underline the verbs in the sentences with blue.

✏️ **Draft Book**
Write two sentences with each of these words: play, watch, paint. Use the words differently in each sentence.

© Carson-Dellosa   CD-4337 Grammar Rules! Grades 1–2   **51**

Page 51 (cont.)
RW: Underline comb, has, likes, want, hangs, bat, turn, and carried with blue.
DB: Answers will vary.
Page 52

In the Beginning — prefixes re- and un-

A prefix is a group of letters added to the beginning of a word. The word the prefix is added to is called the root, or base, word. A prefix changes the meaning of the root word. Two common prefixes are re- and un-. Re- means do again. Un- means not.
example: reorder = order again   The store will reorder the toy.
example: unsafe = not safe   The park is unsafe at night.
Add re to the beginning of each word.

write   rewrite   read   reread

wind   rewind   heat   reheat

Add un to the beginning of each word.

happy   unhappy   known   unknown

opened   unopened   zip   unzip

Use the new words to finish the sentences.

The food is cold. We will have to   reheat   it.

May I have this   unopened   bag of pretzels?

Unzip   your jacket and take it off. It's hot!

We need to   rewind   the videotape.

🔍 **Review Work**
Underline the verbs in the sentences with blue.

✏️ **Draft Book**
Write a sentence with each of the four new words not used in the sentences above.

52 CD-4337 Grammar Rules! Grades 1–2   © Carson-Dellosa

RW: Underline is, will have, may have, unzip, take, is, and need with blue.
DB: Answers will vary.

Page 53

At the End — suffixes -er and -est

A suffix is a group of letters added to the end of a word. The word the suffix is added to is called the root, or base, word. A suffix changes the meaning of the root word. Two common suffixes are -er and -est. -Er means more. -Est means most.
example: younger = more young   Bo is younger than me.
example: youngest = most young   Jill is the youngest girl in class.
Add er and est to the ends of the words.

slow   slower   slowest

small   smaller   smallest

loud   louder   loudest

Add er or est to the end of each word to finish the sentence.

J.J.'s race car is   faster (more fast)   than Joey's.

That is the   softest (most soft)   scarf I've ever felt.

Taylor has the   sweetest (most sweet)   cat in the world!

Is your sand castle   taller (more tall)   than mine?

🔍 **Review Work**
Underline the verbs in the sentences with blue.

✏️ **Draft Book**
Write two sentences with each new -er and -est word.

© Carson-Dellosa   CD-4337 Grammar Rules! Grades 1–2   **53**

RW: Underline is and has with blue.
DB: Answers will vary.

Page 54

Answers will vary. RW: Underline Jenny, Sal, friend, homework, Rianne, Bert, turtle, yard, Marlene, and whistle with yellow. Underline ran, finished, ride, speaks, hear, will work, check, danced, moved, and blow with blue.
DB: Answers will vary.

Page 55

In the Ocean — adverbs

Adverbs are words that tell more about verbs. They tell how something happens. They also tell where something happens.
Circle the adverbs that tell how in the sentences.

Jade swam peacefully in the ocean.

She saw dolphins jumping gracefully.

Fish were gliding lazily through the water.

Something lightly bumped her leg.

Jade screamed loudly.

Her brother Will quickly turned her around.

"It's just me," he said gently.

Color the seashells that contain adverbs that tell where.

here   soon   down   there   above   fast
hard   clumsily   often   inside

🔍 **Review Work**
Underline the nouns in the sentences with yellow. Underline the verbs with blue.

✏️ **Draft Book**
Find a page in your Draft Book with the verbs underlined with blue. Add adverbs to tell where things happened in your sentences.

© Carson-Dellosa   CD-4337 Grammar Rules! Grades 1–2   **55**

RW: Underline Jade, ocean, dolphins, fish, water, something, leg, Jade, brother, and Will with yellow. Underline swam, saw, were gliding, bumped, screamed, turned, is, and said with blue. DB: Answers will vary.
Page 56

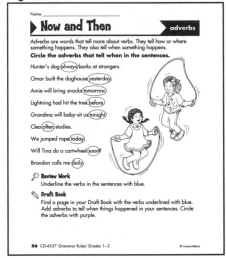

Now and Then — adverbs

Adverbs are words that tell more about verbs. They tell how or where something happens. They also tell when something happens.
Circle the adverbs that tell when in the sentences.

Hunter's dog always barks at strangers.

Omar built the doghouse yesterday.

Amie will bring snacks tomorrow.

Lightning had hit the tree before.

Grandma will baby-sit us tonight.

Cleo often studies.

We jumped rope today.

Will Tina do a cartwheel soon?

Brandon calls me daily.

🔍 **Review Work**
Underline the verbs in the sentences with blue.

✏️ **Draft Book**
Find a page in your Draft Book with the verbs underlined with blue. Add adverbs to tell when things happened in your sentences. Circle the adverbs with purple.

56 CD-4337 Grammar Rules! Grades 1–2   © Carson-Dellosa

RW: Underline barks, built, will bring, had hit, will baby-sit, studies, jumped, will do, and calls with blue. DB: Answers will vary.
Page 57

How, Where, or When — adverbs

Adverbs are words that tell more about verbs. They tell how, where, or when something happens.
What does each adverb tell about the verb? Write how, where, or when on each line.

Ben walked near the beehive.   where

Rita whispered quietly in my ear.   how

Lucy yelled loudly at the game.   how

Mrs. Holmes exercises daily.   when

Jared arrived at the movie early.   when

Adrian's boots are here.   where

Darla pedaled her bike quickly.   how

Hannah often reads books about animals.   when

Drew found the toy inside the cereal box.   where

🔍 **Review Work**
In each sentence, draw an arrow from the adverb to the verb it is telling more about.

✏️ **Draft Book**
Write a story about a toy you would like to find in a cereal box. Include adverbs. Circle the adverbs with purple.

© Carson-Dellosa   CD-4337 Grammar Rules! Grades 1–2   **57**

RW: Draw arrows to walked, whispered, yelled, exercises, arrived, are, pedaled, reads, and found.
DB: Answers will vary.

Page 58
Answers will vary.
RW: Underline crawled, jumped, dragged, landed, chirped, and flew with blue. Draw arrows to these verbs.
DB: Answers will vary.

Page 59

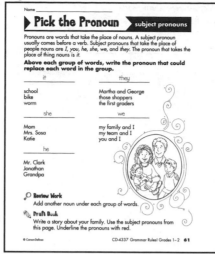

RW: Answers will vary.
DB: Answers will vary.

Page 60

RW: Underline made, saw, has, can roll, is, is, will ride, and do live with blue. Underline omelet, woman, cat, peach, oven, player, car, apartment, and house with yellow.
DB: Answers will vary.

Page 61

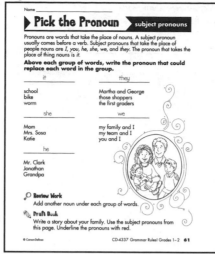

RW: Answers will vary. DB: Answers will vary.
Page 62

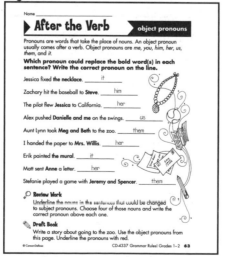

RW: Underline delivered, paid, built, blew, crawled, cleaned, galloped, arrived, and golfed with blue. DB: Answers will vary.
Page 63

RW: Underline Jessica, Zachary, pilot, Alex, Aunt Lynn, paper, Erik, Matt, Stefanie, and game. Answers will vary.
DB: Answers will vary.

Page 64

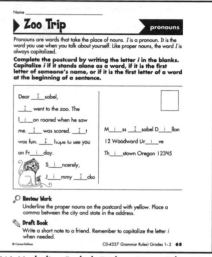

RW: Underline has, has, are, have been, like, like, has, has, gave, gave, has, has, made, made, drove, and drove with blue.
DB: Answers will vary.
Page 65

RW: Underline Isabel, Friday, Jimmy Icko, Miss Isabel Dillon, Woodward Drive, Thistown, and Oregon with yellow. Add a comma between Thistown and Oregon. DB: Answers will vary.
Page 66

RW: Draw a triangle above each proper noun on the postcard that names a place. Draw an X next to each proper noun that names a person. Place a comma between the city and state in the address.

Page 66 (cont.) RW: Draw a triangle above Irwin Avenue, Ingleside, and Nebraska. Draw an X next to Oliver, Will Irstman, and Oliver Lin. DB: Answers will vary.

Page 67

▶ Tiny or Small? `synonyms`

Name _____

Words that mean about the same thing are called synonyms.
example: Quick, swift, and **speedy** mean the same thing as **fast.**
example: Beautiful, attractive, and **lovely** mean the same thing as **pretty.**
The synonyms for *big, happy, little,* **and** *cold* **are mixed up.**
Write the correct synonyms for each word on the lines.

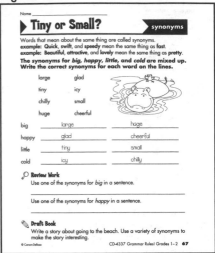

large	glad
tiny	icy
chilly	small
huge	cheerful

big	large	huge
happy	glad	cheerful
little	tiny	small
cold	icy	chilly

🔍 **Review Work**
Use one of the synonyms for *big* in a sentence.
_____
Use one of the synonyms for *happy* in a sentence.
_____

✏️ **Draft Book**
Write a story about going to the beach. Use a variety of synonyms to make the story interesting.

CD-4337 Grammar Rules! Grades 1–2 **67**

RW: Answers will vary. DB: Answers will vary.

Page 68

▶ The Same Stuff `synonyms`

Name _____

Words that mean about the same thing are called synonyms.
Write a synonym from the list for each bold word.

buddies   choose   close   enjoys
fantastic   purchase   race   scream

Lonnie **likes** ice cream. _enjoys_
Please **shut** the door to the ferret cage. _close_
Eva and Marge will **run** to the swings. _race_
Jason will **pick** which book to read. _choose_
I need to **buy** new crayons. _purchase_
That is a **great** painting! _fantastic_
Did you **yell** when you saw the spider? _scream_
Jeanie and Joan are my best **friends.** _buddies_

🔍 **Review Work**
Underline the nouns in the sentences with yellow.

✏️ **Draft Book**
Write a story about playing outside during recess. Use a variety of synonyms from this page to make the story interesting.

68 CD-4337 Grammar Rules! Grades 1–2

RW: Underline Lonnie, ice cream, door, cage, Eva, Marge, swings, Jason, book, crayons, painting, spider, Jeanie, Joan, and friends with yellow. DB: Answers will vary.

Page 69

▶ Opposites `antonyms`

Name _____

Words that mean the opposite of each other are called antonyms.
example: The opposite of **fast** is **slow.**
example: The opposite of **nice** is **mean.**
Circle the word in each group that is the antonym of the first word.

hot	little	(cold)	summer	wet	soft	thirsty	(dry)
long	(short)	red	heavy	asleep	tired	(awake)	reading
cheerful	full	(sad)	happy	stand	eat	drink	(sit)
on	slow	(off)	heavy	tall	(short)	funny	loud
easy	yell	(hard)	blue	dirty	smooth	melted	(clean)

🔍 **Review Work**
Choose a pair of antonyms. Write a sentence using both words.
_____

✏️ **Draft Book**
Write a story about summer vacation. Use a variety of antonyms and other words from this page to make the story interesting.

CD-4337 Grammar Rules! Grades 1–2 **69**

Page 69 (cont.)
RW: Answers will vary.
DB: Answers will vary.

Page 70

▶ Change the Meaning `antonyms`

Name _____

Words that mean the opposite of each other are called antonyms. When a word is replaced by its antonym in a sentence, the meaning of the sentence changes.
example: The pie is **hot.**
example: The pie is **cold.**
Use the words to write an antonym for each bold word.

first   clean   large   hate
quiet   heavy   inside   short

Carlos and I like **loud** music. _quiet_
We played **outside** last night. _inside_
Grace will eat a **small** snack before the game. _large_
Julie, Fred, and Willa **love** chocolate. _hate_
That movie about Alaska was very **long.** _short_
Our **last** day of school will be June 8. _first_
This box of red apples is very **light.** _heavy_
After playing outside, Logan was **dirty.** _clean_

🔍 **Review Work**
Underline the verbs in the sentences with blue. Next to each sentence, write the verb tense: P = present, S = past, or F = future.

✏️ **Draft Book**
Choose a new pair of antonyms. Write a sentence using both words.

70 CD-4337 Grammar Rules! Grades 1–2

RW: Underline like, played, will eat, love, was, will be, is, and was. 1. P 2. S 3. F 4. P 5. S 6. F 7. P 8. S DB: Answers will vary.

Page 71
Draw lines to match blue/blew, sail/sale, eye/I, and mail/male.
RW: sun, ate
DB: Answers will vary.

Page 72
Draw lines to match bear/bare, close/clothes, heal/heel, and berry/bury.
RW: meet, weak
DB: Answers will vary.

Page 73
Draw lines to match pear/pair, flour/flower, one/won, and waist/waste.
RW: dear, plane.
DB: Answers will vary.

Page 74

▶ To, Too, Two `homophones`

Name _____

Homophones are words that sound alike but are spelled differently and have different meanings. *To, too,* and *two* are homophones.
To is used to show direction or purpose.
example: Nell went **to** school.
example: She likes **to** sing.
Too means also or more than enough.
example: Zander wants some milk, **too.**
example: That popcorn has **too** much salt on it!
Two is the number word for the numeral 2.
example: Ramone has **two** sisters.
Write *to, too,* **or** *two* **to finish each sentence.**

Are you checking out _two_ books?
Is your birthday on January 1, _too_ ?
Jackie is going _to_ the ballet program tonight.
The muffins are _too_ hot to eat right now.
Please hand those _two_ papers _to_ Andrew.
I am riding my bike _to_ the park, _too_.
That shirt was _too_ small, so I gave it _to_ Paula.

🔍 **Review Work**
Underline the verbs in the sentences with blue. Circle each form of the linking verb *to be.*

✏️ **Draft Book**
Write one sentence each with *to, too,* and *two.*

74 CD-4337 Grammar Rules! Grades 1–2

RW: Underline are checking, is, is going, are, hand, am riding, and was with blue. Circle are, is, is, are, am, and was.
DB: Answers will vary.

Page 75

▶ I Hear You! `homophones`

Name _____

Homophones are words that sound alike but are spelled differently and have different meanings. *Here/ hear* and *by/buy* are homophones.
example: I am sitting right **here.**
example: I **hear** the radio.
example: Put the flowers **by** the window.
example: Will you **buy** peanuts at the circus?
Write *here, hear, by,* **or** *buy* **to finish each sentence.**

Can you _hear_ the screams of the people on the roller coaster?
Put the bananas right _here_ on the table.
Buy a movie ticket for me, too.
Bart said he could _hear_ the water dripping.
Ryan is standing _by_ the flagpole.
That book was written _by_ Dr. Seuss.
Put the book _here_ and the paper there.
Please _buy_ milk and bread at the store.

🔍 **Review Work**
Circle the articles in the sentences with orange.

✏️ **Draft Book**
Write one sentence each with *here, hear, by,* and *buy.*

CD-4337 Grammar Rules! Grades 1–2 **75**

RW: Circle a and the with orange.
DB: Answers will vary.

Page 76

▶ They're Over There `homophones`

Name _____

Homophones are words that sound alike but are spelled differently and have different meanings. *There, their,* and *they're* are homophones.
There is a place word. **example:** Sit over **there.**
Their is a belonging word. **example:** Shelby is **their** dog.
They're is a contraction for they are. **example:** **They're** playing outside.
Write *there, their,* **or** *they're* **to finish each sentence.**

The long, strong, slithery pythons are over _there_.
They're going to see the huge elephants, snakes, and bears.
The two large, feathered eagles wanted _their_ dinner.
They're planning to find the tropical toucans with the colorful, curved beaks.
There are the funny chimpanzees, gorillas, and orangutans!
The talented chimpanzees can hold, peel, and eat _their_ green bananas.
The zookeeper said that _their_ owls, bats, and foxes are in the nocturnal house, which is over _there_.

🔍 **Review Work**
Circle the adjectives in the sentences. Draw an arrow from each adjective to the noun it describes.

✏️ **Draft Book**
Write one sentence each with *there, their,* and *they're.*

76 CD-4337 Grammar Rules! Grades 1–2

RW: Circle long, strong, slithery, huge, two, large, feathered, their, tropical, colorful, curved, funny, talented, green, their, and nocturnal. Draw arrows to pythons, elephants, eagles, dinner, toucans, beaks, chimpanzees, bananas, owls, bats, foxes, and house.
DB: Answers will vary

Page 77

▶ No, I Don't Know `homophones`

Name _____

Homophones are words that sound alike but are spelled differently and have different meanings. *No/ know* and *write/right* are homophones.
No is the antonym of yes.
example: **No,** you can't do that!
Know is a verb that means to understand.
example: I **know** how to read.
Write is a verb that means to communicate through letters.
example: I can **write** my name.
Right means correct or the opposite of left.
example: That answer is **right.**
example: Hold up your **right** hand.
Write *no, know, write,* **or** *right* **to finish each sentence.**

Do you _know_ if it is snowing in Ohio?
Great job, that answer is _right_ !
Turn _right_ at the corner by Oak Lane.
Rob will _write_ his name at the top of the page.
Is yes or _no_ the _right_ answer?
I _know_ that we will _write_ stories on Monday.

🔍 **Review Work**
Draw an X next to each proper noun that names a person. Draw a triangle above each proper noun that names a place.

✏️ **Draft Book**
Write one sentence each with *no, know, write,* and *right.*

CD-4337 Grammar Rules! Grades 1–2 **77**

RW: Draw an X next to Rob. Draw a triangle above Ohio and Oak Lane.
DB: Answers will vary.

Page 78

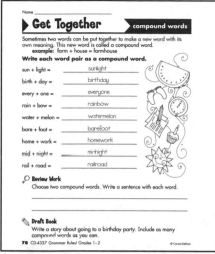

Get Together — compound words

Sometimes two words can be put together to make a new word with its own meaning. This new word is called a compound word.
example: farm + house = farmhouse
Write each word pair as a compound word.

sun + light = sunlight
birth + day = birthday
every + one = everyone
rain + bow = rainbow
water + melon = watermelon
bare + foot = barefoot
home + work = homework
mid + night = midnight
rail + road = railroad

Review Work
Choose two compound words. Write a sentence with each word.

Draft Book
Write a story about going to a birthday party. Include as many compound words as you can.

78 CD-4337 Grammar Rules! Grades 1–2

RW: Answers will vary. DB: Answers will vary.

Page 79

One and One Is Two — compound words

Sometimes two words can be put together to make a new word with its own meaning. This new word is called a compound word.
Write each word pair as a compound word.

after + noon = afternoon
back + yard = backyard
class + mate = classmate
break + fast = breakfast
flash + light = flashlight
oat + meal = oatmeal
pop + corn = popcorn

Use the compound words to finish the sentences.

Nate saw fireflies in his _____
Ricky will need a _____ when he camps outside.
Claire likes to eat _____ at the movies.

Review Work
Underline the other compound words in the sentences.

Draft Book
Write a sentence with each compound word that was not used in one of the sentences above.

© Carson-Dellosa   CD-4337 Grammar Rules! Grades 1–2 79

Compound words in sentences will vary.
RW: Underline fireflies and outside.
DB: Answers will vary.

Page 80

Draw lines to match are not/aren't, were not/weren't, could not/couldn't, did not/didn't, do not/don't, have not/haven't, is not/isn't, and was not/wasn't. 1. aren't 2. didn't 3. isn't 4. don't.
RW: Circle tonight, today, and now with purple.
DB: Answers will vary.

Page 81

Yes, We Will — contractions

A contraction is two words that are put together to make one word. Some of the letters drop out of the second word when the words are joined. An apostrophe takes the place of the dropped letters.
The word will can be combined with pronouns to make contractions.
example: I + will = I'll   example: he + will = he'll
Write the word pair for each contraction.

we'll we will   she'll she will
they'll they will   you'll you will

Write a contraction on the line to finish each sentence.

I will I'll bring in my photo album on Thursday.
My parents decided that we will we'll leave for Niagara Falls tomorrow.
I think you will you'll be able to do at least 20 sit-ups.
Maria's friends think they will they'll go to see the fireworks.
Theo said he will he'll play his tuba this afternoon.

Review Work
Underline the nouns in the sentences with yellow. Draw an X next to each proper noun that names a person. Draw a triangle above each proper noun that names a place.

Draft Book
Write a sentence with each contraction on this page.

© Carson-Dellosa   CD-4337 Grammar Rules! Grades 1–2 81

RW: Underline album, Thursday, parents, Niagara Falls, sit-ups, Maria, friends, fireworks, Theo, tuba, and afternoon. Draw an X next to Maria and Theo. Draw a triangle above Niagara Falls.
DB: Answers will vary.

Page 82

Won't — contractions

A contraction is two words that are put together to make one word. Some of the letters drop out of the second word when the words are joined. An apostrophe takes the place of the dropped letters.
The verb will can be combined with the word not to make won't.
Underline the contraction in each sentence. Rewrite each sentence by changing the contraction to the pronoun and adding won't. The first one has been done for you.

We'll go swimming today.
We won't go swimming today.
Fiona said she'll order apple pie.
Fiona said she won't order apple pie.
Next year, he'll be in fourth grade.
Next year, he won't be in fourth grade.
You'll need to help shovel the snow.
You won't need to help shovel the snow.
They'll clear the table and do the dishes.
They won't clear the table and do the dishes.

Review Work
What two words make up the contraction won't?
will   not

Draft Book
Write a story about washing the dishes. Use the contraction won't.

82 CD-4337 Grammar Rules! Grades 1–2   © Carson-Dellosa

DB: Answers will vary

Page 83

Draw lines to match he is/he's, I would/I'd, she is/she's, you have/you've, we are/we're, he would/he'd, they have/they've, I am/I'm, what is/what's, you are/you're, I have/I've, and let us/let's.
RW: Circle is, is, are, are, am, is, and are.
DB: Answers will vary.

Page 84

Think About It — contractions

A contraction is two words that are put together to make one word. Some of the letters usually drop out of the second word when the words are joined. An apostrophe takes the place of the dropped letters.
Write a contraction on the line to finish the sentence.

Jill won't climb that enormous tree.
     will not
The sign says you'll need a green ticket to get in.
               you will
I think we're eating a hot dinner soon.
         we are
_____ What's the recipe for bread dough?
        What is
That wasn't the fourth bell.
      was not
_____ She'd ridden the yellow bus to school.
        She had
_____ Who's feeding the two hamsters this week?
        Who is

Review Work
Circle the adjectives in the sentences. Draw an arrow from each adjective to the noun it describes.

Draft Book
Write a story about climbing a tree. Use contractions in your story.

84 CD-4337 Grammar Rules! Grades 1–2   © Carson-Dellosa

RW: Circle enormous, green, hot, bread, fourth, yellow, and two. Draw arrows to tree, ticket, dinner, dough, bell, bus, and hamsters.
DB: Answers will vary.

Page 85

Beginning Letters — sentences

A sentence is a group of words that tells a complete thought. A sentence always starts with an uppercase letter.
Rewrite the sentences. Start each sentence with an uppercase letter. Circle the uppercase letter at the beginning of each sentence.

i like studying grammar.
(I) like studying grammar.
mary will underline nouns with yellow.
(M)ary will underline nouns with yellow.
sandy and Kit underline verbs with blue.
(S)andy and Kit underline verbs with blue.
janice circled the first noun in the sentence.
(J)anice circled the first noun in the sentence.

Review Work
Underline the verbs in the sentences with blue. Next to each sentence, write the verb tense: P = present, S = past, or F = future.

Draft Book
Write four sentences about reading your favorite book. Start each sentence with an uppercase letter. Circle the uppercase letter at the beginning of each sentence.

© Carson-Dellosa   CD-4337 Grammar Rules! Grades 1–2 85

RW: Underline like, will underline, underline, and circled with blue. 1. P 2. F 3. P 4. S
DB: Answers will vary

Page 86

One Day — sentences

A sentence is a group of words that tells a complete thought. A sentence always starts with an uppercase letter.
Circle the first letter of each sentence. Write an uppercase letter next to each lowercase letter that needs to be changed.

I (i)n the afternoon, we learn about science.
I (i) get to school at 8:45 A.M.
I (i) sit down at my desk.
O (o)livia helps with the calendar.
M (m)y pencil breaks during math.
M (m)iss Acker reads a great book.
T (t)he class eats lunch.
W (w)e clean out our messy desks.
R (r)yan picks me up after school.
M (m)iss Acker will teach us about volcanoes tomorrow.

Review Work
Underline the verbs in the sentences with blue. Write an F next to the sentence that is written in future tense.

Draft Book
Write three sentences about your favorite season. Start each sentence with an uppercase letter. Circle the uppercase letter at the beginning of each sentence.

86 CD-4337 Grammar Rules! Grades 1–2   © Carson-Dellosa

Page 86 (cont.)
RW: Underline learn, get, sit, helps, breaks, reads, eats, clean, picks, and will teach with blue. Write an F next to the last sentence.
DB: Answers will vary.

Page 87

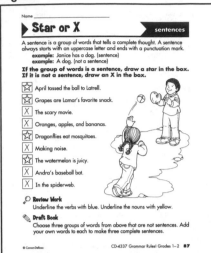

Star or X — sentences

A sentence is a group of words that tells a complete thought. A sentence always starts with an uppercase letter and ends with a punctuation mark.
example: Janice has a dog. (sentence)
example: A dog. (not a sentence)

If the group of words is a sentence, draw a star in the box. If it is not a sentence, draw an X in the box.

☆ April tossed the ball to Latrell.
☆ Grapes are Lamar's favorite snack.
✗ The scary movie.
✗ Oranges, apples, and bananas.
☆ Dragonflies eat mosquitoes.
✗ Making noise.
☆ The watermelon is juicy.
✗ Andra's baseball bat.
✗ In the spiderweb.

RW: Underline tossed, are, eat, making, and is with blue. Underline April, ball, Latrell, Lamar, grapes, snack, movie, oranges, apples, bananas, dragonflies, mosquitoes, noise, watermelon, Andra, bat, and spiderweb with yellow. DB: Answers will vary.

Page 88

Find the Stars — sentences

A sentence is a group of words that tells a complete thought. A sentence always starts with an uppercase letter and ends with a punctuation mark.
example: Is that Quincy's fish? (sentence)
example: Is that? (not a sentence)

If the group of words is a sentence, draw a star in the box. If it is not a sentence, draw an X in the box.

☆ When will Ross call me?
✗ Write it?
✗ Is Helene?
☆ Will you climb the ladder?
☆ Where is the bird going?
✗ In the cave?
☆ What kind of juice do you like?
☆ Who can help me open the jar?
✗ Will the?

RW: Underline me, it, you, you, and me with red. DB: Answers will vary

Page 89
Answers will vary.

Page 90

Snow Day — statements

There are four types of sentences. A telling, or declarative, sentence tells something. A declarative sentence can also be called a statement. A declarative sentence always ends with a period.
Rewrite the declarative sentences. Start each sentence with an uppercase letter and put a period at the end.

snowmen melt in the sun
Snowmen melt in the sun.

mittens keep her hands warm
Mittens keep her hands warm.

julian packs snow into snowballs
Julian packs snow into snowballs.

zoe makes tunnels in the snowbank
Zoe makes tunnels in the snowbank.

travis and Stephen build an igloo
Travis and Stephen build an igloo.

Review Work
Underline the nouns in the sentences with yellow.

Draft Book
Write four declarative sentences about playing in the snow. Start each sentence with an uppercase letter. End each sentence with a period.

RW: Underline snowmen, sun, mittens, hands, Julian, snow, snowballs, Zoe, tunnels, snowbank, Travis, Stephen, and igloo with yellow. DB: Answers will vary.

Page 91

That Does It — statements

There are four types of sentences. A telling, or declarative, sentence tells something. A declarative sentence can also be called a statement. A declarative sentence always ends with a period.
Use the words to finish the declarative sentences. End each sentence with a period.

bread   letters   marshmallows   music
stories   teeth   pictures   time

A piano makes _____ music.
An oven bakes _____ bread.
Your brother reads you _____ stories/letters.
A dentist takes care of _____ teeth.
The clock tells _____ time.
I like writing _____ stories/letters.
That fire roasts _____ marshmallows.
A crayon colors _____ pictures.

Review Work
Circle the uppercase letter at the beginning of each sentence. Circle the period at the end of each sentence.

Draft Book
Write three declarative sentences about roasting marshmallows. Start each sentence with an uppercase letter. End each sentence with a period.

RW: Circle the beginning uppercase letters and ending periods. DB: Answers will vary

Page 92

I Want to Know — questions

There are four types of sentences. An asking, or interrogative, sentence asks a question. An interrogative sentence can also be called a question. An interrogative sentence always ends with a question mark.
Rewrite the interrogative sentences. Start each sentence with an uppercase letter and put a question mark at the end.

who got the book
Who got the book?

where is my friend
Where is my friend?

what is that bug called
What is that bug called?

why are you laughing
Why are you laughing?

when are we leaving
When are we leaving?

Review Work
In the sentences, circle each form of the linking verb to be.

Draft Book
Write four interrogative sentences about going to lunch. Start each sentence with an uppercase letter. End each sentence with a question mark.

RW: Circle is, is, are, and are.
DB: Answers will vary.

Page 93

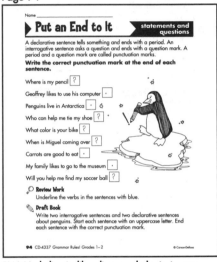

Ask a Question — questions

There are four types of sentences. An asking, or interrogative, sentence asks a question. An interrogative sentence can also be called a question. An interrogative sentence always ends with a question mark.
Use the words to finish the interrogative sentences. End each sentence with a question mark.

crayons   bag   desk   sneeze
lunch   fit   dot   sticky

Is the glue _____ sticky?
Do elephants _____ sneeze?
Do your new shoes _____ fit?
Is an ant as small as a _____ dot?
What will you eat for _____ lunch?
Will you color with the _____ crayons?
Why are you sitting at my _____ desk?
What is in your _____ bag?

Review Work
Circle the uppercase letter at the beginning of each sentence. Circle the question mark at the end of each sentence.

Draft Book
Write three interrogative sentences about elephants. Start each sentence with an uppercase letter. End each sentence with a question mark.

RW: Circle the beginning uppercase letters and ending question marks. DB: Answers will vary.

Page 94

Put an End to It — statements and questions

A declarative sentence tells something and ends with a period. An interrogative sentence asks a question and ends with a question mark. A period and a question mark are called punctuation marks.
Write the correct punctuation mark at the end of each sentence.

Where is my pencil ?
Geoffrey likes to use his computer .
Penguins live in Antarctica .
Who can help me tie my shoe ?
What color is your bike ?
When is Miguel coming over ?
Carrots are good to eat .
My family likes to go to the museum .
Will you help me find my soccer ball ?

Review Work
Underline the verbs in the sentences with blue.

Draft Book
Write two interrogative sentences and two declarative sentences about penguins. Start each sentence with an uppercase letter. End each sentence with the correct punctuation mark.

RW: Underline is, likes, live, can help, is, is, are, likes, and will help with blue. DB: Answers will vary.

Page 95

Once Upon a Tree — statements and questions

A declarative sentence tells something and ends with a period. An interrogative sentence asks a question and ends with a question mark. A period and a question mark are called punctuation marks.
Write the correct punctuation mark at the end of each sentence.

A tree grows in our backyard .
Are the leaves on the branches important to the tree ?
The leaves make food for the tree .
Leaves also store food .
What do the roots do ?
The roots pull in water and minerals .
Where do seeds come from ?
Seeds form in the seed pods .
Do trees have flowers ?
Trees have flowers or cones .

Review Work
Underline the nouns in the sentences with yellow.

Draft Book
Write three interrogative sentences and three declarative sentences about trees. Start each sentence with an uppercase letter. End each sentence with the correct punctuation mark.

RW: Underline tree, backyard, leaves, branches, tree, leaves, food, tree, leaves, food, roots, roots, water, minerals, seeds, seeds, seed pods, trees, flowers, trees, flowers, and cones with yellow. DB: Answers will vary.

Page 96

> ▶ **Where Are They?** | statements and questions
>
> A declarative sentence tells something and ends with a period. An interrogative sentence asks a question and ends with a question mark. A period and a question mark are called punctuation marks.
> **Write the correct punctuation mark at the end of each sentence.**
>
> Where do monarch butterflies come from [?]
> Monarch butterflies are from Mexico [.]
> Where do dolphins live [?]
> Dolphins live in the ocean [.]
> Where do elephants live [?]
> Elephants are from Asia and Africa [.]
> Where can spiders be found [?]
> Spiders live nearly everywhere on Earth [.]
>
> 🔍 **Review Work**
> Underline the nouns in the sentences with yellow. Draw a triangle above each proper noun that names a place.
>
> ✏️ **Draft Book**
> Choose a topic and write three interrogative sentences and three declarative sentences about it. Start each sentence with an uppercase letter. End each sentence with the correct punctuation mark.
>
> 96 CD-4337 Grammar Rules! Grades 1–2 © Carson-Dellosa

RW: Underline butterflies, butterflies, Mexico, dolphins, dolphins, ocean, elephants, elephants, Asia, Africa, spiders, spiders, and Earth. Draw a triangle above Mexico, Asia, Africa, and Earth. DB: Answers will vary.

Page 97

> ▶ **What?** | statements and questions
>
> A declarative sentence tells something and ends with a period. An interrogative sentence asks a question and ends with a question mark. A period and a question mark are called punctuation marks.
> **Look at each answer and write a question that could be asked. Start each question with an uppercase letter and end with a question mark. The first one has been done for you.**
>
> Question: What does four plus five equal?
> Answer: Four plus five equals nine.
>
> Question: Do you have a pencil?
> Answer: Yes, I have my pencil right here.
>
> Question: What time is it?
> Answer: It is 11:30 A.M.
>
> Question: What is an interrogative sentence?
> Answer: An interrogative sentence is a sentence that asks a question.
>
> Question: Are you ready to go to lunch?
> Answer: Yes, we are ready to go to lunch.
>
> 🔍 **Review Work**
> Circle the first letter of each sentence. Circle the ending punctuation marks. Draw a star next to each interrogative sentence.
>
> ✏️ **Draft Book**
> Choose a topic and write your own set of interrogative and declarative sentences. Start each sentence with an uppercase letter. End each sentence with the correct punctuation mark.
>
> © Carson-Dellosa CD-4337 Grammar Rules! Grades 1–2 97

RW: Circle beginning uppercase letters and ending punctuation. Draw a star next to sentences labeled Question. DB: Answers will vary.

Page 98

> ▶ **Wow!** | exclamations
>
> There are four types of sentences. An exclamatory sentence is used when the writer wants to show strong feelings. An exclamatory sentence always ends with an exclamation mark.
> **Rewrite the exclamatory sentences. Start each sentence with an uppercase letter and put an exclamation mark at the end.**
>
> i did not break that window
> I did not break that window!
>
> this is the best gift I've ever gotten
> This is the best gift I've ever gotten!
>
> i see a shooting star
> I see a shooting star!
>
> ouch, that really hurt
> Ouch, that really hurt!
>
> 🔍 **Review Work**
> Choose one sentence. Draw a check mark next to it. If that sentence was an answer, write a follow-up question.
>
> ✏️ **Draft Book**
> Write four exclamatory sentences about the best gift you've ever received. Start each sentence with an uppercase letter. End each sentence with an exclamation mark.
>
> 98 CD-4337 Grammar Rules! Grades 1–2 © Carson-Dellosa

Page 98 (cont.)
RW: Answers will vary. DB: Answers will vary.

Page 99

> ▶ **Great!** | exclamations
>
> There are four types of sentences. An exclamatory sentence is used when the writer wants to show strong feelings. An exclamatory sentence always ends with an exclamation mark.
> **Use the words to finish the exclamatory sentences. End each sentence with an exclamation mark.**
>
> good   foot   test   beach
> building   snake   glass   school
>
> This pie tastes _____ good!
> We are going to the _____ beach!
> That _____ snake _____ scared me!
> I did not break that _____ glass!
> That _____ building _____ is tall!
> Don't step on my _____ foot!
> I passed the _____ test!
> I can't wait for _____ school _____ to start!
>
> 🔍 **Review Work**
> Circle the uppercase letter at the beginning of each sentence. Circle the exclamation mark at the end of each sentence.
>
> ✏️ **Draft Book**
> Write three exclamatory sentences. Start each sentence with an uppercase letter. End each sentence with an exclamation mark.
>
> © Carson-Dellosa CD-4337 Grammar Rules! Grades 1–2 99

RW: Circle beginning uppercase letters and ending exclamation marks. DB: Answers will vary.

Page 100

> ▶ **Now Do This** | commands
>
> There are four types of sentences. An imperative sentence tells you what to do or makes a request. An imperative sentence can also be called a command. An imperative sentence usually ends with a period.
> **Rewrite the imperative sentences. Start each sentence with an uppercase letter and put a period at the end.**
>
> clean your room
> Clean your room.
>
> stop tickling me
> Stop tickling me.
>
> take the dog for a walk before dinner
> Take the dog for a walk before dinner.
>
> wait until the bell rings before you leave
> Wait until the bell rings before you leave.
>
> turn off the television
> Turn off the television.
>
> 🔍 **Review Work**
> Underline the verbs in the sentences with blue.
>
> ✏️ **Draft Book**
> Choose a topic and write five imperative sentences. Start each sentence with an uppercase letter. End each sentence with a period.
>
> 100 CD-4337 Grammar Rules! Grades 1–2 © Carson-Dellosa

RW: Underline clean, stop, take, wait, and turn with blue. DB: Answers will vary.

Page 101

> ▶ **Together Again** | commands
>
> There are four types of sentences. An imperative sentence tells you what to do or makes a request. An imperative sentence can also be called a command. An imperative sentence usually ends with a period.
> **Match the two halves of each command. Write the sentences correctly. Start each sentence with an uppercase letter and end with a period.**
>
> use a crayon — to eat that candy
> wait until later — before it stops ringing
> answer the phone — to color the picture
> take the ice — on this paper
> write the story — out of the freezer
>
> Use a crayon to color the picture.
> Wait until later to eat that candy.
> Answer the phone before it stops ringing.
> Take the ice out of the freezer.
> Write the story on this paper.
>
> 🔍 **Review Work**
> Underline the imperative sentences in the directions.
>
> ✏️ **Draft Book**
> Write five imperative sentences. Start each sentence with an uppercase letter. End each sentence with a period.
>
> © Carson-Dellosa CD-4337 Grammar Rules! Grades 1–2 101

RW: Underline all three direction sentences. DB: Answers will vary.

Page 102

> ▶ **Beginning and End** | sentence types
>
> A sentence is a group of words that tells a complete thought. A sentence always starts with an uppercase letter and ends with a punctuation mark.
> **Cross out the first letter in each sentence and write the uppercase letter next to it. Circle the correct punctuation mark at the end.**
>
> D d̶oes Angie know how to read . ! (?)
> E e̶mory baked a chocolate cake (.) ! ?
> J j̶ustin turned on the computer (.) ! ?
> E e̶at your lunch (.) ! ?
> T t̶he snake is loose (!) . ?
> T t̶urn off the light (.) ! ?
> W w̶hen will the parade start . ! (?)
> H h̶elp, my hand is stuck . (!) ?
>
> 🔍 **Review Work**
> Count how many of each type of sentence are shown.
> declarative: 2   interrogative: 2
> exclamatory: 2   imperative: 2
>
> ✏️ **Draft Book**
> Find a full page of writing in your Draft Book. Circle the punctuation marks. If a punctuation mark is not correct, fix it.
>
> 102 CD-4337 Grammar Rules! Grades 1–2 © Carson-Dellosa

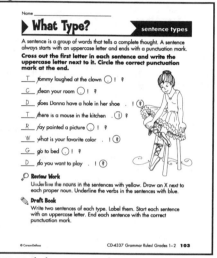

DB: Answers will vary.

Page 103

> ▶ **What Type?** | sentence types
>
> A sentence is a group of words that tells a complete thought. A sentence always starts with an uppercase letter and ends with a punctuation mark.
> **Cross out the first letter in each sentence and write the uppercase letter next to it. Circle the correct punctuation mark at the end.**
>
> T t̶ommy laughed at the clown (.) ! ?
> C c̶lean your room (.) ! ?
> D d̶oes Donna have a hole in her shoe . ! (?)
> T t̶here is a mouse in the kitchen . (!) ?
> R r̶ay painted a picture (.) ! ?
> W w̶hat is your favorite color . ! (?)
> G g̶o to bed (.) ! ?
> D d̶o you want to play . ! (?)
>
> 🔍 **Review Work**
> Underline the nouns in the sentences with yellow. Draw an X next to each proper noun. Underline the verbs in the sentences with blue.
>
> ✏️ **Draft Book**
> Write two sentences of each type. Label them. Start each sentence with an uppercase letter. End each sentence with the correct punctuation mark.
>
> CD-4337 Grammar Rules! Grades 1–2 103

RW: Underline Tommy, clown, room, Donna, hole, shoe, mouse, kitchen, Ray, picture, color, and bed with yellow. Draw an X next to Tommy, Donna, and Ray. Underline laughed, clean, does have, is, painted, is, go, and do want with blue. DB: Answers will vary.

Page 104

> ▶ **The Right Ending** | sentence types
>
> There are four types of sentences.
> 1 - declarative: tells something, ends with a period
> 2 - interrogative: asks a question, ends with a question mark
> 3 - exclamatory: shows strong feelings, ends with an exclamation point
> 4 - imperative: gives a command or request, usually ends with a period
> **Decide which type each sentence is. Write the number in the box before the sentence. Write the correct punctuation mark in the box after the sentence.**
>
> [2] What time are we going to the pool [?]
> [4] Finish your work [.]
> [2] How far is Nevada from Iowa [?]
> [2] Why do worms eat dirt [?]
> [1] Lebron has a bunk bed [.]
> [3] Wow, that idea is fantastic [!]
> [4] Get the map [.]
> [1] I like spaghetti [.]
>
> 🔍 **Review Work**
> Underline the nouns in the sentences with yellow.
>
> ✏️ **Draft Book**
> Write two sentences of each type. Label them. Start each sentence with an uppercase letter. End each sentence with the correct punctuation mark.
>
> 104 CD-4337 Grammar Rules! Grades 1–2 © Carson-Dellosa

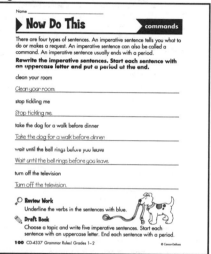

RW: Underline time, pool, work, Nevada, Iowa, worms, dirt, Lebron, bed, idea, map, and spaghetti with yellow.
DB: Answers will vary.

Page 105

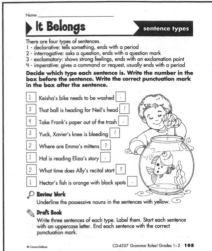

It Belongs — sentence types

There are four types of sentences.
1 - declarative: tells something, ends with a period
2 - interrogative: asks a question, ends with a question mark
3 - exclamatory: shows strong feelings, ends with an exclamation point
4 - imperative: gives a command or request, usually ends with a period

Decide which type each sentence is. Write the number in the box before the sentence. Write the correct punctuation mark in the box after the sentence.

1 Keisha's bike needs to be washed .
3 That ball is heading for Neil's head !
4 Take Frank's paper out of the trash .
3 Yuck, Xavier's knee is bleeding !
2 Where are Emma's mittens ?
1 Hal is reading Eliza's story .
2 What time does Ally's recital start ?
1 Hector's fish is orange with black spots .

Review Work
Underline the possessive nouns in the sentences with yellow.

Draft Book
Write three sentences of each type. Label them. Start each sentence with an uppercase letter. End each sentence with the correct punctuation mark.

CD-4337 Grammar Rules! Grades 1–2 **105**

RW: Underline Keisha's, Neil's, Frank's, Xavier's, Emma's, Eliza's, Ally's, and Hector's with yellow.
DB: Answers will vary.

Page 106

Separate Them — commas

A comma is a type of punctuation mark used to separate a group of three or more words in a list or series.
example: Sal ate **grapes**, **yogurt**, and **soup** for lunch.

Put commas between the words in each series.

Tim went fishing on Wednesday, Friday, Saturday, and Monday.

Ahmad, Spencer, Reese, and Jeremy played soccer.

Garrett, Faith, Justin, and I drove to the festival.

The fair had rides, food, animals, and games.

George likes to play with Zack, Tommy, Cole, and me.

Antoine's favorite subjects are math, reading, and science.

Perry has relatives in Florida, Indiana, and Tennessee.

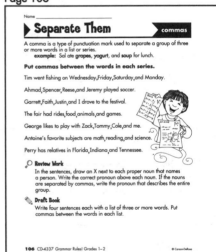

Review Work
In the sentences, draw an X next to each proper noun that names a person. Write the correct pronoun above each noun. If the nouns are separated by commas, write the pronoun that describes the entire group.

Draft Book
Write four sentences each with a list of three or more words. Put commas between the words in each list.

106 CD-4337 Grammar Rules! Grades 1–2

RW: Draw an X next to Tim, Ahmad, Spencer, Reese, Jeremy, Garrett, Faith, Justin, George, Zack, Tommy, Cole, Antoine, and Perry. 1. He 2. They 3. We 5. He, us 6. His 7. He/She
DB: Answers will vary.

Page 107

What Type of Word? — commas

A comma is a type of punctuation mark used to separate a group of three or more words in a list or series.
example: Austin, Javier, and Owen went hiking. (nouns)
example: Mia can **run**, **hop**, and **jump**. (verbs)
example: Throw that **skinny**, **little**, **broken** crayon away. (adjectives)
example: Rabbits hopped **over**, **under**, and **between** the plants. (adverbs)

Circle the commas in the sentences. Write what type of words (noun, verb, adjective, or adverb) the commas separate in each sentence.

Tyesha walked quickly, quietly, and carefully away from the beehive.

adverb

Molly bikes, hikes, and swims when she goes camping.

verb

We saw anteaters, zebras, jaguars, and bats at the zoo.

noun

I like fresh, hot, salty, buttery popcorn.

adjective

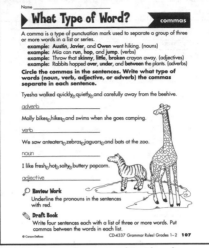

Review Work
Underline the pronouns in the sentences with red.

Draft Book
Write four sentences each with a list of three or more words. Put commas between the words in each list.

CD-4337 Grammar Rules! Grades 1–2 **107**

RW: Underline she, we, and I with red.
DB: Answers will vary.

Page 108

How Many? — commas

A comma is a type of punctuation mark used to separate a group of three or more words in a list or series.
Circle the commas in the sentences. Answer the questions.

We bought bananas, cherry tomatoes, beans, and onions at the market.

How many things did we buy? 4

Lynda, Myong, and Joanne made beaded bracelets.

How many girls made beaded bracelets? 3

Brady walked, hopped, crawled, and skipped through the obstacle course.

How many things did Brady do? 4

Richard saw starfish, eels, clams, fish, and spiny lobsters at the aquarium.

How many types of things did Richard see? 5

Pack your toothbrush, sleeping bag, pillow, and pajamas.

How many things should you pack? 4

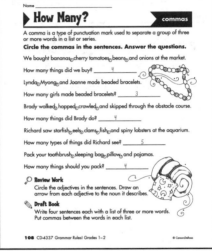

Review Work
Circle the adjectives in the sentences. Draw an arrow from each adjective to the noun it describes.

Draft Book
Write four sentences each with a list of three or more words. Put commas between the words in each list.

108 CD-4337 Grammar Rules! Grades 1–2

RW: Circle cherry, beaded, beaded, obstacle, and spiny. Draw arrows to tomatoes, bracelets, bracelets, course, and lobsters.
DB: Answers will vary.

Page 109

Commas in Dates — commas

A comma is a type of punctuation mark used to separate a group of three or more words in a list or series. Commas are also used in certain dates to separate the day of the week, the month and date, and the year.
example: Monday, August 11
example: Monday, August 11, 2003
example: August 11, 2003

Some dates don't need commas.
example: August 11   example: August 2003

Put commas where they are needed in the dates. Write an uppercase letter above each lowercase letter that needs to be changed.

T N
tuesday, november 12, 1996

T M
thursday, march 20

D
december 30, 2004

J
july 1885

W A
wednesday, april 24, 2002

S
september 4, 1984

D
dustin's birthday is january 21.

N A
nina started second grade on august 27, 1999.

K J
karen will graduate in june 2010.

I M A
ian was born on monday, august 26, 1991.

Review Work
Choose one sentence. Rewrite it as a question.

Draft Book
Write three sentences with dates. Put commas where they are needed.

CD-4337 Grammar Rules! Grades 1–2 **109**

RW: Answers will vary.
DB: Answers will vary

Page 110

Dinnertime — quotation marks

Quotation marks are a type of punctuation mark used to go around the words that people say.
example: "You did a great job!" said Bruce.
Put quotation marks around the words that people are saying in the sentences.

"May I have some chips?" asked Liv.

Mom replied, "No, we're going to eat dinner soon."

"How about some grapes?" questioned Darian.

"How about helping me finish dinner?" suggested Mom.

"Can I get a vegetable plate ready? I can do that!" exclaimed Liv.

Mom smiled. "That would be a big help," Liv.

"I'll set the table," said Darian.

"Thanks! Dinner is almost ready," said Mom.

"All done," said Darian.

"Me, too!" shouted Liv.

Review Work
In the sentences, underline the verbs that are used in place of the verb *said*.

Draft Book
Write a story about a conversation you had with a friend or family member. Put quotation marks around the words that people said.

110 CD-4337 Grammar Rules! Grades 1–2

RW: Underline asked, replied, questioned, suggested, exclaimed, smiled, and shouted.
DB: Answers will vary.

Page 111

Who Said That? — quotation marks

Quotation marks are a type of punctuation mark used to go around the words that people say.
example: "Can I borrow a pencil?" asked Hayden.
Put quotation marks around the words that people are saying in the sentences.

"It's a secret," whispered Donovan.

"Don't touch that!" screeched Alysa.

Brenda yelled, "I've got the ball!"

"I'm glad that's done," sighed Ms. Horn.

"I understand now!" exclaimed Sean.

"This is the best burger ever," stated Wesley.

"Yes, I can help you with that," replied Ernesto.

"What is your name?" asked Georgia.

"You have to push this button," explained Colton.

"This is fun," said Holly.

Review Work
In the sentences, underline the verbs that are used in place of the verb *said*.

Draft Book
Choose five verbs from above that are used in place of the verb *said*. Write a sentence with each verb. Put quotation marks around the words people say.

CD-4337 Grammar Rules! Grades 1–2 **111**

RW: Underline whispered, screeched, yelled, sighed, exclaimed, stated, replied, asked, and explained. DB: Answers will vary.

Page 112

Dear Friend — friendly letters

A friendly letter has five parts: date, greeting, body, closing, and signature. A comma is needed after the greeting and closing.

August 5, 2002 ← date
Dear Grandma, ← greeting
Thank you for the game! It is the one I wanted. I hope we can play it together when you come over on Sunday. ← body
Love, ← closing
Annabelle ← signature

Fill in the missing parts of the friendly letter. Label each part.

_____, 2003 ← date
Dear _____ ← greeting
You are invited to a picnic! Let me know if you can come. I hope to see you there. ← body
Sincerely, ← closing
_____ ← signature

Review Work
Underline the pronouns in the friendly letters with red.

Draft Book
Write a letter to a friend. Include the five parts of a friendly letter. Remember to use punctuation marks where they are needed.

112 CD-4337 Grammar Rules! Grades 1–2